Collins School Atlas

Published by Collins
An imprint of HarperCollins Publishers
Westerhill Road
Bishopbriggs
Glasgow G64 2QT
www.harpercollins.co.uk

Fourth edition 2016

© HarperCollins Publishers 2016
Maps © Collins Bartholomew Ltd 2016

Collins ® is a registered trademark of HarperCollins Publishers Ltd

A catalogue record for this book is available from the British Library.

ISBN 978-0-00-814676-4

10 9 8 7 6 5 4 3 2

Printed in Hong Kong

All mapping in this atlas is generated from Collins Bartholomew digital databases. Collins Bartholomew, the UK's leading independent geographical information supplier, can provide a digital, custom, and premium mapping service to a variety of markets. For further information:
Tel: +44 (0) 208 307 4515
e-mail: collinsbartholomew@harpercollins.co.uk

Visit our websites at:
www.collins.co.uk
www.collinsbartholomew.com

If you would like to comment on any aspect of this book, please contact us at the above address or online.
e-mail: collinsmaps@harpercollins.co.uk

The Solar System

The Solar System is the Sun and the many objects that orbit it.
These objects include eight planets, at least five dwarf planets and
countless asteroids, meteoroids and comets. Orbiting some of the
planets and dwarf planets are over 160 moons. The Sun keeps its
surrounding objects in its orbit by its pull of gravity which has an
influence for many millions of kilometres.

Saturn

Jupiter

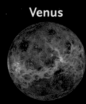

Asteroid
Belt

Mars

Earth

Venus

Mercury

Sun

The Sun

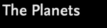

Diameter
1 391 016 km
Circumference
4 370 000 km
Average temperature
5504 °C
Rotation about axis
(measured at its equator)
25 Earth days 9 hours

The Planets

	Mercury	Venus	Earth	Mars
Diameter	4900 km	12 100 km	12 700 km	6779 km
Circumference	15 300 km	38 000 km	40 000 km	21 300 km
Distance from Sun	58 million km	108 million km	150 million km	228 million km
Length of year	88 Earth days	244 Earth days 17 hours	365 days 6 hours	687 Earth days
Length of day	59 Earth days	243 Earth days	23 hours 56 minutes	24 hours 37 minutes

	Jupiter	Saturn	Uranus	Neptune
Diameter	143 000 km	116 500 km	50 700 km	49 200 km
Circumference	450 000 km	366 000 km	159 000 km	154 700 km
Distance from Sun	778 million km	1427 million km	2871 million km	4498 million km
Length of year	11 Earth years 314 days	29 Earth years	84 Earth years	165 Earth years
Length of day	9 hours 55 minutes	10 hours 39 minutes	17 hours 14 minutes	16 hours 7 minutes

Neptune

Uranus

The seasons

The Earth's axis is tilted from perpendicular therefore different parts of the globe are orientated towards the Sun at different times of the year. The four seasons, Spring, Summer, Autumn and Winter are a result of this.

March 21

The Sun is overhead at the Equator and both the North and South poles are equidistant from the Sun. The Northern Hemisphere experiences Spring for three months while the Southern Hemisphere experiences Autumn.

December 21

The Sun is overhead at the Tropic of Capricorn. The North Pole is inclined away from the Sun and is in total darkness. The Northern Hemisphere experiences Winter for three months while the Southern Hemisphere experiences Summer.

Sun

June 21

The Sun is overhead at the Tropic of Cancer. The North Pole is inclined towards the Sun and has 24 hour daylight. The Northern Hemisphere experiences Summer for three months while the Southern Hemisphere experiences Winter.

September 21

The Sun is overhead at the Equator and both the North and South poles are equidistant from the Sun. The Northern Hemisphere experiences Autumn for three months while the Southern Hemisphere experiences Spring.

Day and night

The Earth turns round on its axis every 23 hours 56 minutes and it is this rotation that is responsible for the daily cycles of day and night. At any one moment in time, one half of the Earth is in sunlight, while the other half, facing away from the Sun, is in darkness. As the Earth rotates it also creates the apparent movement of the Sun from east to west across the sky.

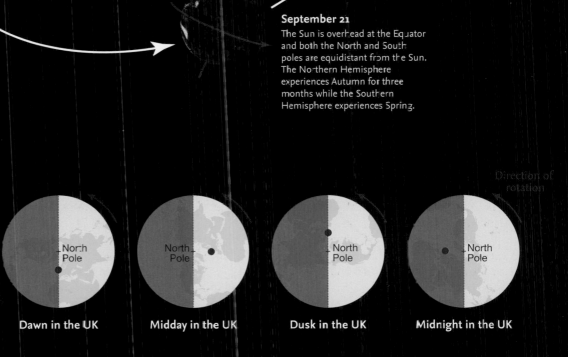

Direction of rotation

| Dawn in the UK | Midday in the UK | Dusk in the UK | Midnight in the UK |

North Pole · North Pole · North Pole · North Pole

Using atlas maps

An atlas includes different kinds of maps and diagrams. The different parts of an atlas page are shown on the map below which is a reduced version of page 32 in the atlas. In order to understand maps it is important to understand the labels and information which appear on each page. The example below is a reference map which shows a variety of information such as settlement, communications, the physical landscape and political borders.
In this atlas there are also many thematic maps which give information on one or two special topics. Maps A, B, C and D on page 5 are typical examples of four different types of thematic map.

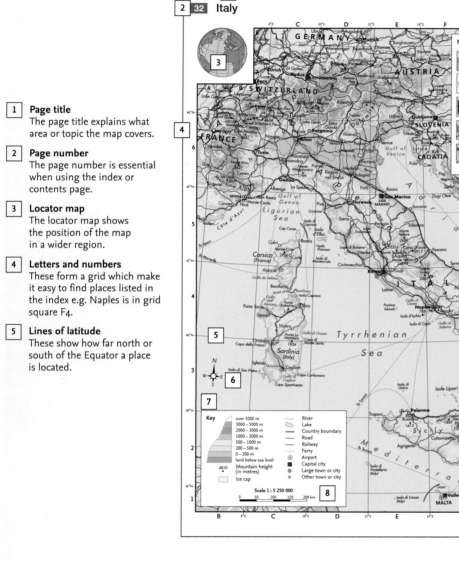

1   **Page title**
The page title explains what area or topic the map covers.

2   **Page number**
The page number is essential when using the index or contents page.

3   **Locator map**
The locator map shows the position of the map in a wider region.

4   **Letters and numbers**
These form a grid which make it easy to find places listed in the index e.g. Naples is in grid square F4.

5   **Lines of latitude**
These show how far north or south of the Equator a place is located.

6   **Compass**
The compass shows the direction of north, south, east and west. Maps are usually drawn with north at the top of the page.

7   **Key box**
Every map has a key which explains the symbols used on the map. The use of symbols on the maps in this atlas are explained in more detail on page 8.

8   **Scale bar and ratio scale**

9   **Projection note**

10   **Lines of longitude**
These show how far east or west of the Greenwich Meridian a place is located.

11   **Facts box**
Information in the Facts Box is subdivided into various categories. An icon (or symbol) identifies each of the categories which are explained below.

Facts box

The information listed in the **Facts about...** box is explained below.

Landscape: Indicates the area and highest point.

Population: Lists the total population and the average number of people living in one square kilometre.

Settlement: Shows the percentage of the population living in cities and towns. The main towns and cities are also listed.

Land use: Main crops grown and the main industries in the region are identified here.

Development indicators: Four indicators are shown here.

Life expectancy: The number of years a newborn child can expect to survive.

GNI per capita: The annual value of production of goods and services of a country, per person.

Primary school enrolment: The total of all ages enrolled at primary level as a percentage of primary age children.

Access to safe water: Percentage of the population with reasonable access to sufficient safe water.

A Political map

Map A uses different colours to show clearly the shape of each country. A line is used to represent the international boundary around each country. It is possible to see the relative areas of the countries. Capital cities and other major cities are shown by symbols on a Political map.

C Relief map

Map C shows the height of the land. Areas which are the same height above sea level are shown in the same colour. Lowland is shown in green and the highest mountain areas in brown or purple. The landscape features are named on a relief map and symbols are used to show the main mountain peaks. From this map we can see that Kilimanjaro is the highest peak in Africa.

B Rainfall map

The colours on Map B represent areas which have the same range of annual rainfall. From this type of map it is possible to find the wettest or driest region in a country. Rainfall maps are often accompanied by climate graphs such as the one shown below.

D Population map

The colours used on this map show the distribution of the population in the rural areas. Different sizes of dot show the distribution of cities and towns. Together the different colours and different size dots show where most of the people of Kenya live.

Graphs

Information in this atlas is often presented as a graph or diagram. Three examples of graphs used are shown to the right.
Pie graphs are circles divided into segments to show percentage values.
Bar graphs can be used to compare quantities between different topics or countries.
Climate graphs are a combination of bars and lines.

Pie graph

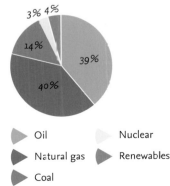

- Oil
- Natural gas
- Coal
- Nuclear
- Renewables

Bar graph

Number of immigrants (thousands)

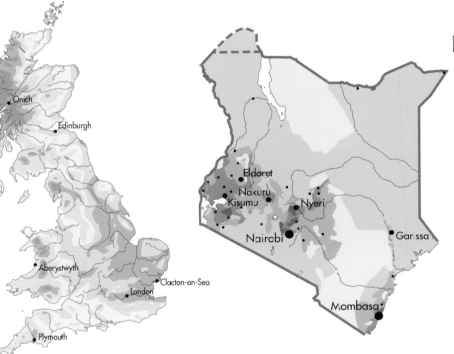

Germany
UK
France
Italy
Spain

Climate graph

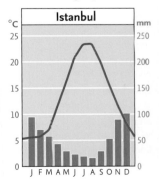

Istanbul

Latitude and longitude

Lines of latitude are imaginary lines which run in an east-west direction around the globe. They run parallel to each other and are measured in degrees, written as °. The most important line of latitude is the **Equator**, 0°. All other lines of latitude have a value between 0° and 90° north or south of the Equator. 90° north is the North Pole and, 90° south, the South Pole.

Lines of longitude are imaginary lines which run in a north-south direction between the **North Pole** and the **South Pole**. The most important line of longitude is 0°, the **Greenwich Meridian**, which runs through the Greenwich Observatory in London. Exactly opposite the Greenwich Meridian on the other side of the world, is the 180° line of longitude. All other lines of longitude are measured in degrees east or west of 0°.

When both lines of latitude and longitude are drawn on a map they form a grid. It is easy to find a place on the map if the latitude and longitude values are known. The point of intersection of the line of latitude and the line of longitude locates the place exactly.

The Equator can be used to divide the globe into two halves. Land north of the Equator is the **Northern Hemisphere.** Land south of the Equator is the **Southern Hemisphere.** The 0° and 180° lines of longitude can also be used to divide the globe into two halves, the **Western** and **Eastern Hemispheres.** Together, the Equator and 0° and 180°, divide the world into four areas, for example, North America is in the Northern Hemisphere and the Western Hemisphere.

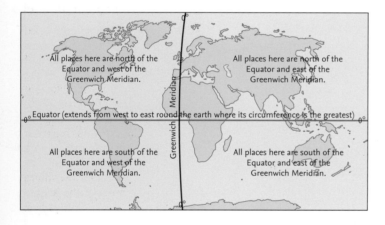

Using scale

The **scale** of each map in this atlas is shown in two ways:

  1. The ratio scale is written, for example, as 1 : 1 000 000. This means that one unit of measurement on the map represents 1 000 000 of the same unit on the ground.
  e.g. **Scale 1 : 1 000 000**

  2. The line or **bar scale** shows the scale as a line with the distance on the ground marked at intervals along the line.

Different scales

The three maps to the right cover the same area of the page but are at different scales. Map A is a large scale map which shows a small area in detail. Map C is a small scale map which means it shows a larger area in the same space as Map A, however in much less detail. The area of Map A is highlighted on maps B and C. As the scale ratio increases the map becomes smaller.

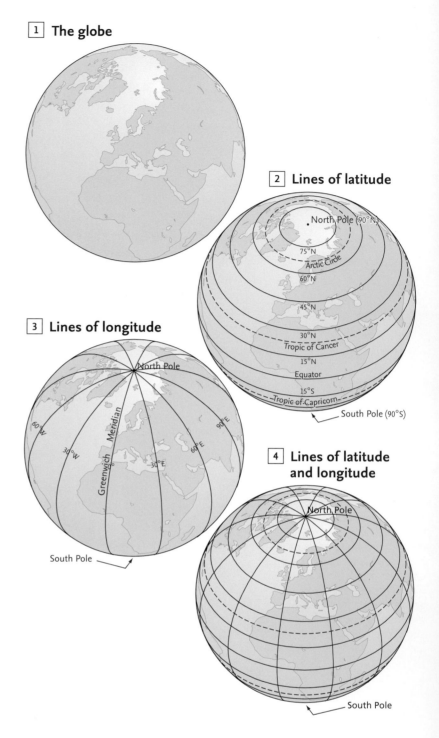

Mapping the world

To show the world on a flat map we need to peel the surface of the globe and flatten it out. There are many different methods of altering the shape of the Earth so that it can be mapped on an atlas page. These methods are called **projections**.

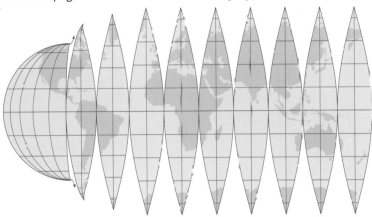

Projections

Map projections change the shape and size of the continents and oceans. The projection used for world maps in this atlas is called Eckert IV. How the world map looks, depends on which continents are at the centre of the map.

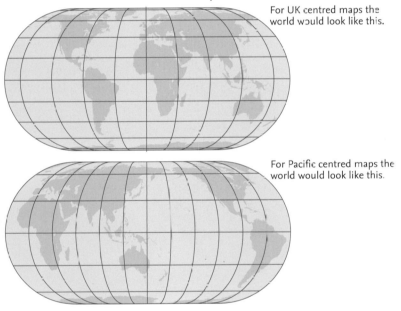

For UK centred maps the world would look like this.

For Pacific centred maps the world would look like this.

Measuring distance

The scale of a map can also be used to work out how far it is between two places. In the example below, the straight line distance between Brasília and Salvador on the map of Brazil is 7 cm. The scale of the map is 1 : 15 000 000. Therefore 7 cm on the map represents 7 x 15 000 000 cm or 105 000 000 cm on the ground. Converted to kilometres this is 1050 km. The real distance between Brasília and Salvador is therefore 1050 km on the ground.

Scale 1 : 15 000 000

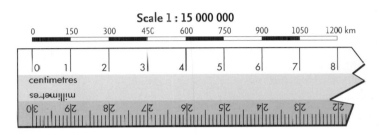

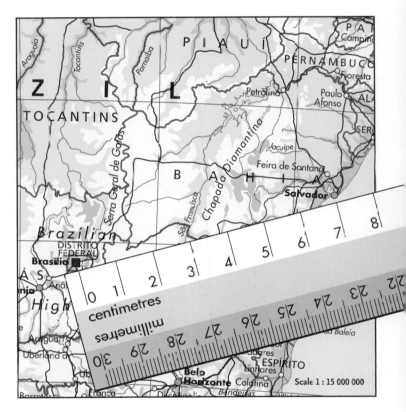

Map B

Scale 1 : 5 000 000

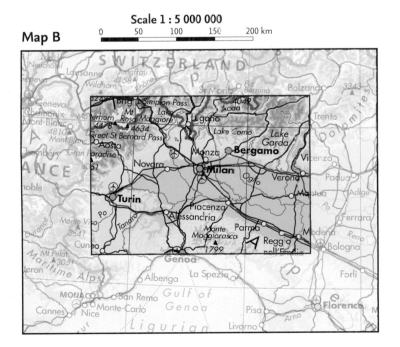

Map C

Scale 1 : 15 000 000

Symbols

Maps use **symbols** to show the location of a feature and to give information about that feature. The symbols used on each map in this atlas are explained in the **key** to each map.

Symbols used on maps can be dots, diagrams, lines or area colours. They vary in colour, size and shape. The numbered captions to the map below help explain some of the symbols used on the maps in this atlas.

Different styles of type are also used to show differences between features, for example, country names are shown in large bold capitals, small water features, rivers and lakes in small italics.

Using grids

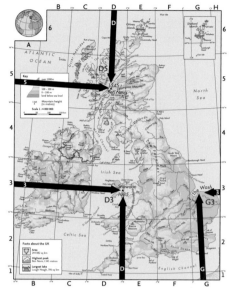

The map on the left shows the British Isles. Lines of latitude and longitude are numbered in 2° intervals in the map frame. These form a **grid** on the map. Large letters and numbers, together known as **alphanumerics,** are used to label the horizontal and vertical columns made by the grid.

The alphanumerics can be used to identify the **grid square** in which a feature is located, for example:

Ben Nevis is in D5,
Snowdon in D3,
The Wash in G3.

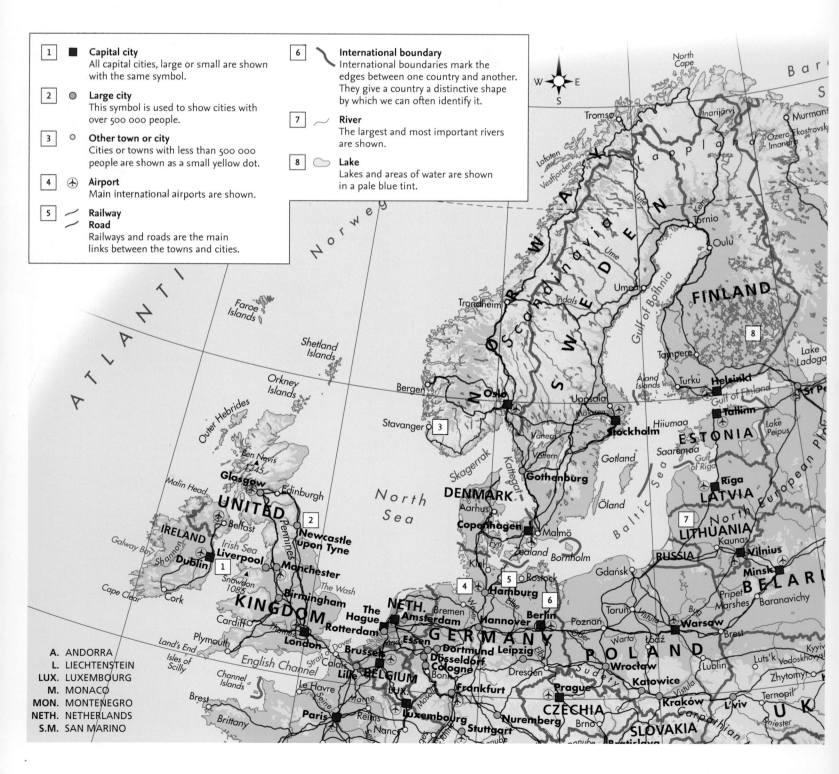

1 ■ **Capital city** All capital cities, large or small are shown with the same symbol.	**6** ∿ **International boundary** International boundaries mark the edges between one country and another. They give a country a distinctive shape by which we can often identify it.	
2 ● **Large city** This symbol is used to show cities with over 500 000 people.	**7** ⌒ **River** The largest and most important rivers are shown.	
3 ○ **Other town or city** Cities or towns with less than 500 000 people are shown as a small yellow dot.	**8** ⬭ **Lake** Lakes and areas of water are shown in a pale blue tint.	
4 ✈ **Airport** Main international airports are shown.		
5 ∼ **Railway** ∼ **Road** Railways and roads are the main links between the towns and cities.		

A. ANDORRA
L. LIECHTENSTEIN
LUX. LUXEMBOURG
M. MONACO
MON. MONTENEGRO
NETH. NETHERLANDS
S.M. SAN MARINO

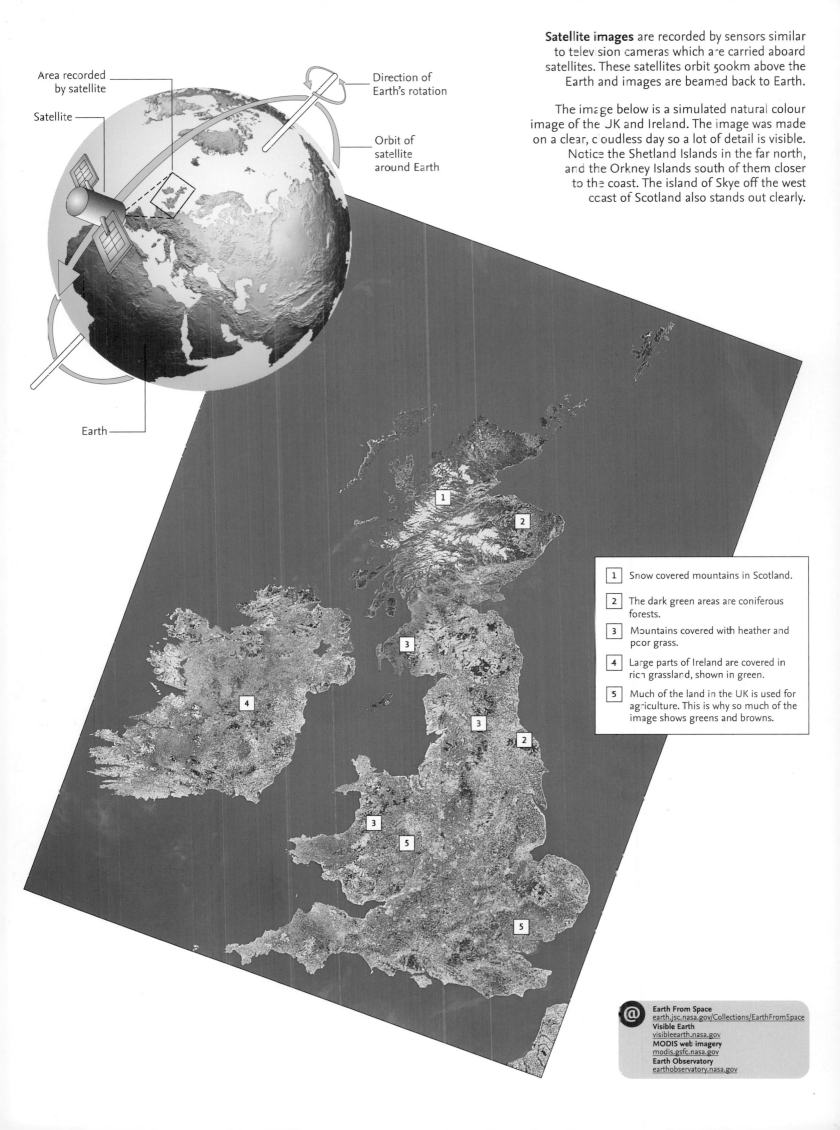

Satellite images are recorded by sensors similar to television cameras which are carried aboard satellites. These satellites orbit 500km above the Earth and images are beamed back to Earth.

The image below is a simulated natural colour image of the UK and Ireland. The image was made on a clear, cloudless day so a lot of detail is visible. Notice the Shetland Islands in the far north, and the Orkney Islands south of them closer to the coast. The island of Skye off the west coast of Scotland also stands out clearly.

Area recorded by satellite

Satellite

Direction of Earth's rotation

Orbit of satellite around Earth

Earth

1	Snow covered mountains in Scotland.
2	The dark green areas are coniferous forests.
3	Mountains covered with heather and poor grass.
4	Large parts of Ireland are covered in rich grassland, shown in green.
5	Much of the land in the UK is used for agriculture. This is why so much of the image shows greens and browns.

Earth From Space
earth.jsc.nasa.gov/Collections/EarthFromSpace
Visible Earth
visibleearth.nasa.gov
MODIS web imagery
modis.gsfc.nasa.gov
Earth Observatory
earthobservatory.nasa.gov

What is GIS?

GIS stands for **Geographic Information System.** A GIS is a set of tools which can be used to collect, store, retrieve, modify and display spatial data. Spatial data can come from a variety of sources including existing maps, satellite imagery, aerial photographs or data collected from GPS (Global Positioning System) surveys.

GIS links this information to its real world location and can display this in a series of layers which you can then choose to turn off and on or to combine. GIS is often associated with maps, however there are 3 ways in which a GIS can be applied to work with spatial information, and together they form an intelligent GIS:

1. The database view – the geographic database (or Geodatabase) is a structured database which stores and describes the geographic information.

2. The map view – a set of maps can be used to view data in different ways using a variety of symbols and layers as shown on the illustration on the right.

3. The model view – A GIS is a set of tools that create new geographic datasets from existing datasets. These tools take information from existing datasets, apply rules and write results into new datasets.

Why use GIS?

A GIS can be used in many ways to help people and businesses solve problems, find patterns, make decisions or to plan for future developments. A map in a GIS can let you find places which contain some specific information and the results can then be displayed on a map to provide a clear simple view of the data.

For example you might want to find out the number of houses which are located on a flood plain in an area prone to flooding. This can be calculated and displayed using a GIS and the results can then be used for future planning or emergency provision in the case of a flood.

A company could use a GIS to view data such as population figures, income and transport in a city centre to plan where to locate a new business or where to target sales. Mapping change is also possible within a GIS. By mapping where and how things move over a period of time, you can gain insight into how they behave. For example, a meteorologist might study the paths of hurricanes to predict where and when they might occur in the future.

GIS USERS

The National Health Service	Environmental Agencies
The Police	Councils
Estate Agents	Supermarkets
Government Agencies	Insurance Companies
Schools	Banks
Emergency Services	Holiday Companies
The Military	Mapping Agencies

GIS layers

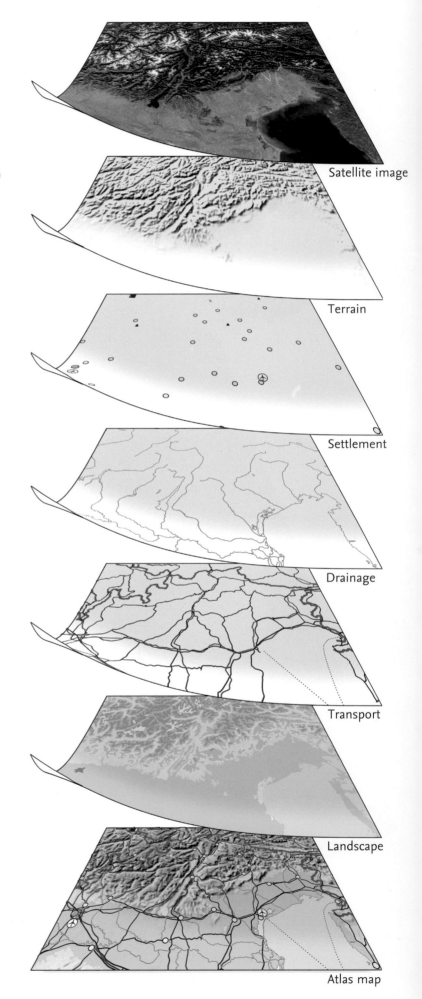

Satellite image

Terrain

Settlement

Drainage

Transport

Landscape

Atlas map

Terrain

This map shows the relief of the country, and highlights the areas which are hilly in contrast to flatter areas. Relief can be represented in a variety of ways – contours and area colours can both show the topography. This terrain map uses shading which makes the hilly areas obvious.

Energy sources

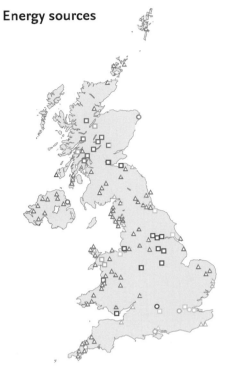

This map illustrates the location of energy sources in the UK using point symbols. Each point symbol contains coordinate information and represents the different types of energy sources, for example the blue triangles show the location of wind farms. Points can be used to represent a variety of features such as banks, schools or shopping centres.

Transportation

Roads shown here have been split into two categories, Motorways in green and Primary Roads in red, and these have been attributed with their road number. This is a road network using linear symbols. Rivers and railways could also be shown like this.

Land use

This Land Use map illustrates the different ways in which the land is used in areas across the UK. Each area is coloured differently depending on the type of land use. Areas in yellow are dominated by farms which grow crops, whereas urban areas are shown in red and forests in green. This map is used to show agricultural land use, but a similar map could be used to show different types of soils for example.

Regional migration

Graphs can be used on maps as a type of point symbol, and are an effective way of representing changes over time. This map has been divided into the regions of Britain and shows the number of people moving in and out of each region. The orange bar shows the number of people (in thousands) moving into an area, and the green bar shows the number of people moving out.

Population distribution

Population distribution can be shown on a map by using different colours for each category. This map uses 3 categories and each shows the number of people in a square kilometre. The yellow areas contain less than 10 people per square km; the light orange areas have 10 – 150, whilst the dark orange areas contain over 150 people per square km. The dark orange areas therefore have the highest population density.

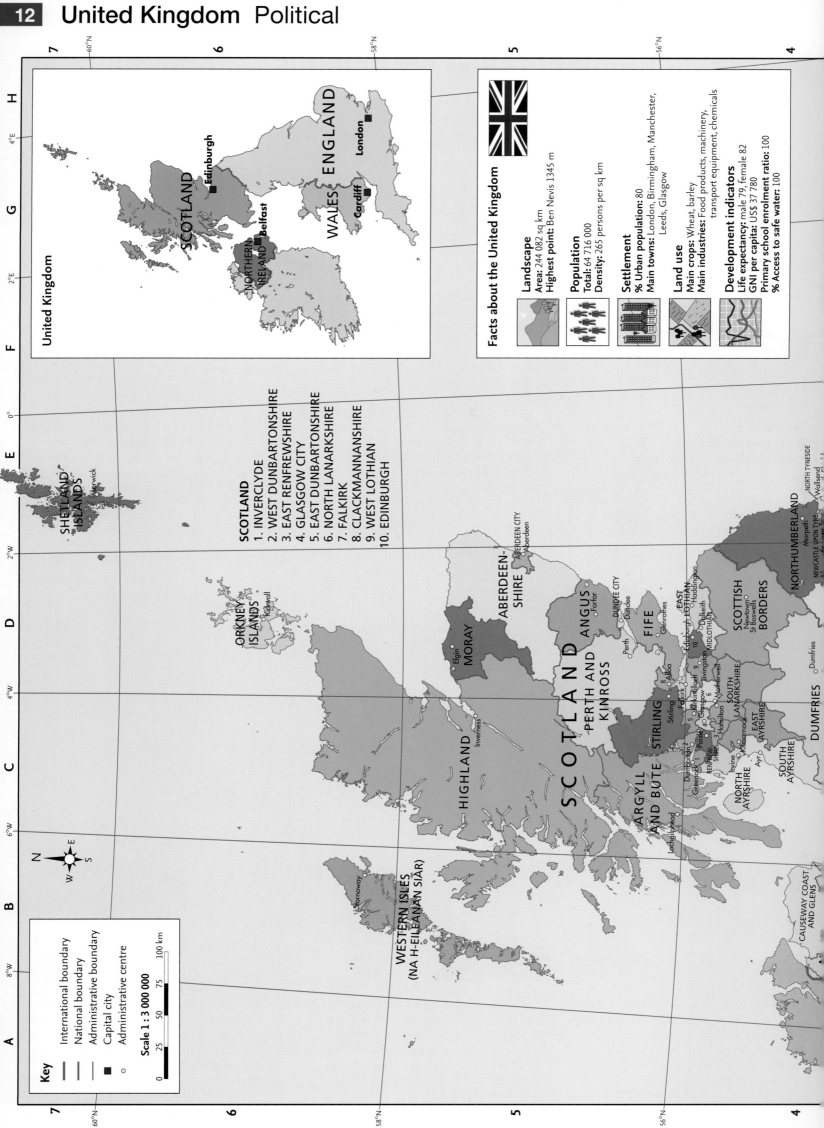

United Kingdom

SCOTLAND
ENGLAND
WALES
NORTHERN IRELAND
Edinburgh
Belfast
London
Cardiff

Facts about the United Kingdom

Landscape
Area: 244 082 sq km
Highest point: Ben Nevis 1345 m

Population
Total: 64 716 000
Density: 265 persons per sq km

Settlement
% Urban population: 80
Main towns: London, Birmingham, Manchester, Leeds, Glasgow

Land use
Main crops: Wheat, barley
Main industries: Food products, machinery, transport equipment, chemicals

Development indicators
Life expectancy: male 79, female 82
GNI per capita: US$ 37 780
Primary school enrolment ratio: 100
% Access to safe water: 100

SCOTLAND
1. INVERCLYDE
2. WEST DUNBARTONSHIRE
3. EAST RENFREWSHIRE
4. GLASGOW CITY
5. EAST DUNBARTONSHIRE
6. NORTH LANARKSHIRE
7. FALKIRK
8. CLACKMANNANSHIRE
9. WEST LOTHIAN
10. EDINBURGH

SHETLAND ISLANDS
Lerwick

ORKNEY ISLANDS
Kirkwall

WESTERN ISLES
(NA H-EILEANAN SIAR)
Stornoway

HIGHLAND
Inverness

MORAY
Elgin

ABERDEEN-SHIRE
ABERDEEN CITY
Aberdeen

SCOTLAND

PERTH AND KINROSS
Perth

ANGUS
Forfar

DUNDEE CITY
Dundee

STIRLING
Stirling

FIFE
Glenrothes

EAST LOTHIAN
Haddington
Dalkeith
MIDLOTHIAN

ARGYLL AND BUTE
Lochgilphead

SCOTTISH BORDERS
Newtown
St Boswells

Alloa
Falkirk
Kirkintilloch
Livingston
Edinburgh
8
7
5
10
9

Dumbarton
Greenock
1
2
Paisley
Renfrew
3
4
Glasgow
6
Hamilton
Motherwell
SOUTH LANARKSHIRE
RENFREW-SHIRE

NORTH AYRSHIRE
Irvine
Kilmarnock
EAST AYRSHIRE
Ayr
SOUTH AYRSHIRE

DUMFRIES
Dumfries

NORTHUMBERLAND
Morpeth
NEWCASTLE UPON TYNE
NORTH TYNESIDE
Wallsend

CAUSEWAY COAST AND GLENS

Key
International boundary
National boundary
Administrative boundary
■ Capital city
○ Administrative centre

Scale 1 : 3 000 000
0 25 50 75 100 km

N
W   E
S

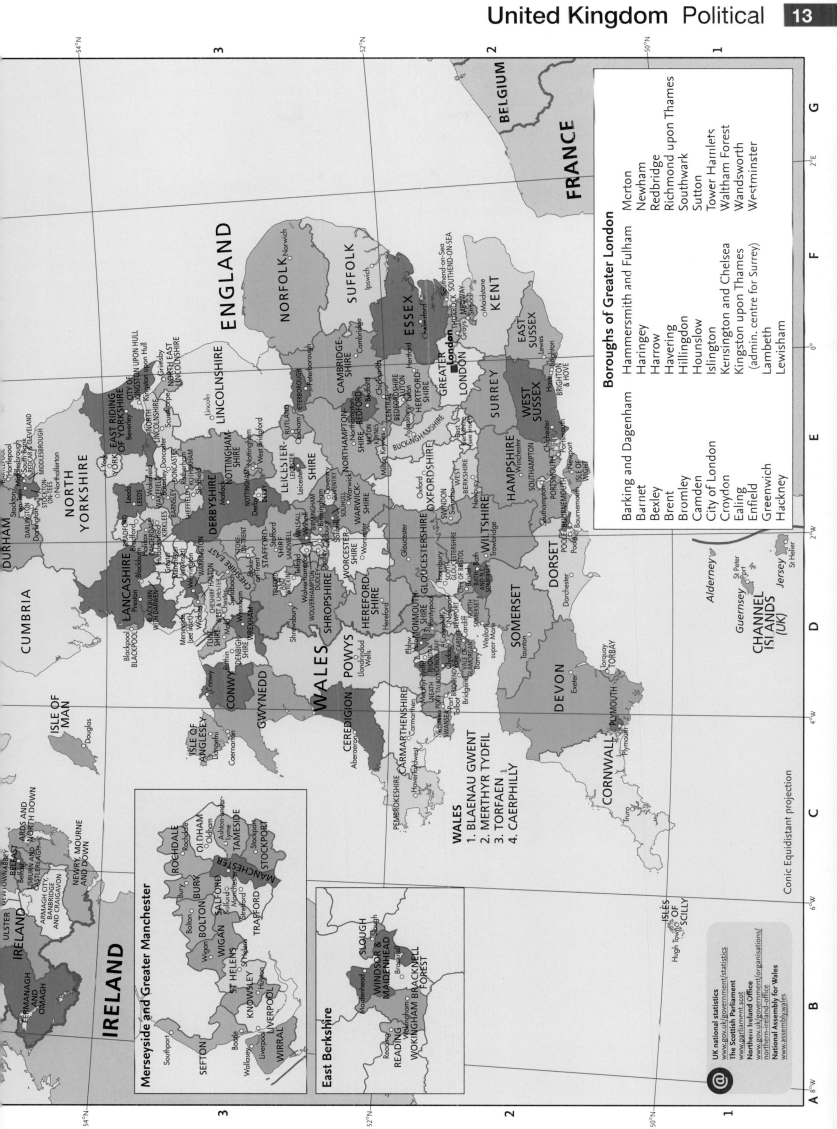

ATLANTIC

OCEAN

over 1000m
500 – 1000 m
200 – 500 m
100 – 200 m
0 – 100 m
land below sea level

▲ 1345   Mountain height
(in metres)

Scale 1 : 4 000 000

North

Sea

Irish
Sea

Celtic Sea

English Channel

Lambert Azimuthal Equal Area projection

Shetland
Islands

Facts about the UK

Area
244 082 sq km

Highest peak
Ben Nevis, 1345 metres

Largest lake
Lough Neagh, 396 sq km

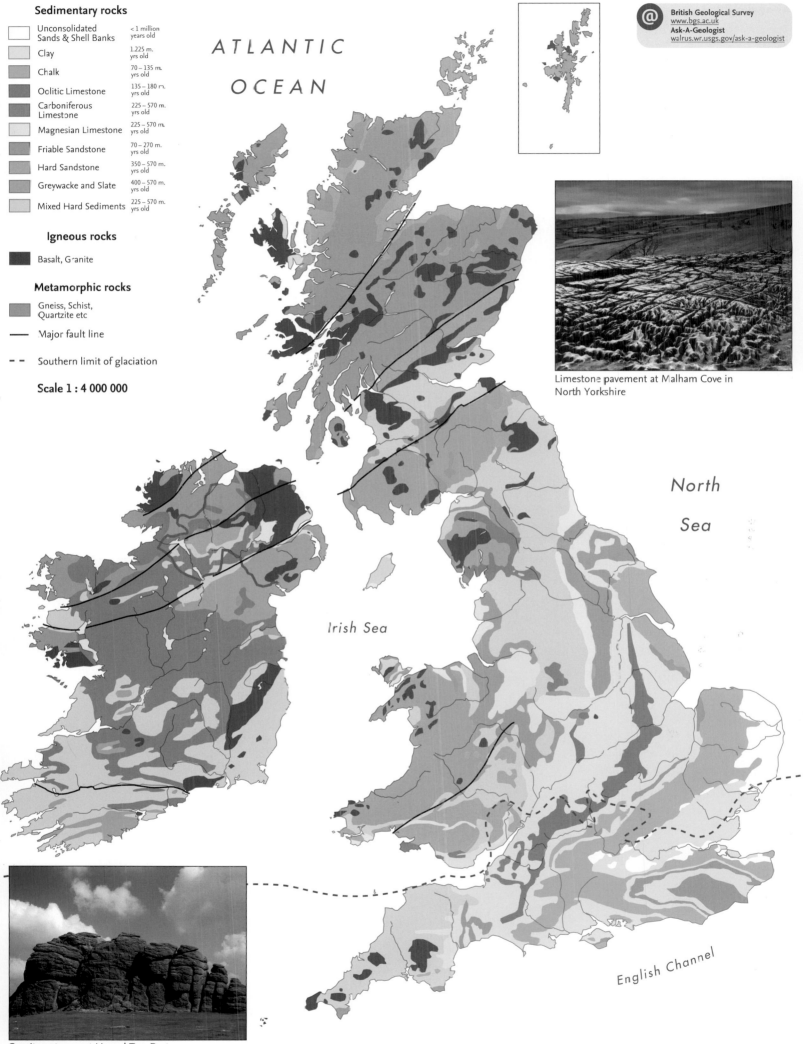

Sedimentary rocks

	Unconsolidated Sands & Shell Banks	< 1 million years old
	Clay	1.225 m. yrs old
	Chalk	70 – 135 m. yrs old
	Oolitic Limestone	135 – 180 m. yrs old
	Carboniferous Limestone	225 – 570 m. yrs old
	Magnesian Limestone	225 – 570 m. yrs old
	Friable Sandstone	70 – 270 m. yrs old
	Hard Sandstone	350 – 570 m. yrs old
	Greywacke and Slate	400 – 570 m. yrs old
	Mixed Hard Sediments	225 – 570 m. yrs old

Igneous rocks

Basalt, Granite

Metamorphic rocks

Gneiss, Schist, Quartzite etc

—— Major fault line

- - - Southern limit of glaciation

Scale 1 : 4 000 000

ATLANTIC OCEAN

North Sea

Irish Sea

English Channel

@ British Geological Survey
www.bgs.ac.uk
Ask-A-Geologist
walrus.wr.usgs.gov/ask-a-geologist

Limestone pavement at Malham Cove in North Yorkshire

Granite outcrops at Hound Tor, Dartmoor

Annual rainfall

There is little variation between winter and summer. The highest rainfall is in the west where winds from the sea blow against the mountains and hills. Central and eastern areas are more sheltered and have lower rainfall.

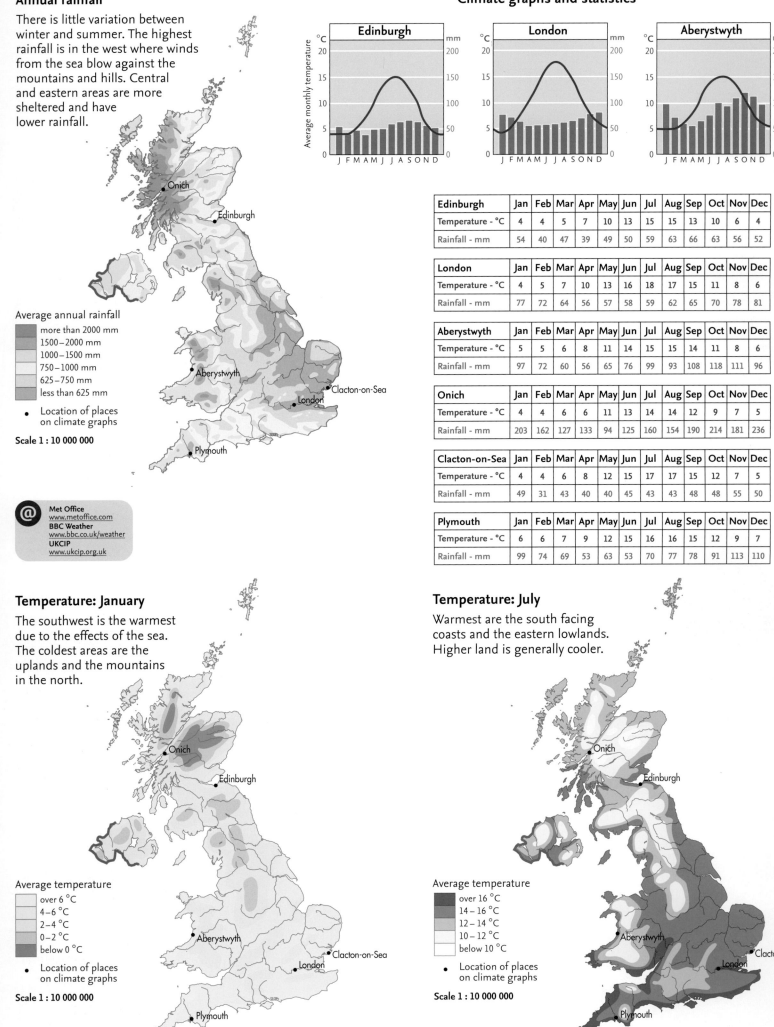

Average annual rainfall

- more than 2000 mm
- 1500–2000 mm
- 1000–1500 mm
- 750–1000 mm
- 625–750 mm
- less than 625 mm

● Location of places on climate graphs

Scale 1 : 10 000 000

@ **Met Office**
www.metoffice.com
BBC Weather
www.bbc.co.uk/weather
UKCIP
www.ukcip.org.uk

Climate graphs and statistics

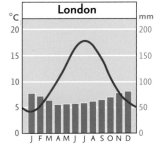

Edinburgh	Jan	Feb	Mar	Apr	May	Jun	Jul	Aug	Sep	Oct	Nov	Dec
Temperature - °C	4	4	5	7	10	13	15	15	13	10	6	4
Rainfall - mm	54	40	47	39	49	50	59	63	66	63	56	52

London	Jan	Feb	Mar	Apr	May	Jun	Jul	Aug	Sep	Oct	Nov	Dec
Temperature - °C	4	5	7	10	13	16	18	17	15	11	8	6
Rainfall - mm	77	72	64	56	57	58	59	62	65	70	78	81

Aberystwyth	Jan	Feb	Mar	Apr	May	Jun	Jul	Aug	Sep	Oct	Nov	Dec
Temperature - °C	5	5	6	8	11	14	15	15	14	11	8	6
Rainfall - mm	97	72	60	56	65	76	99	93	108	118	111	96

Onich	Jan	Feb	Mar	Apr	May	Jun	Jul	Aug	Sep	Oct	Nov	Dec
Temperature - °C	4	4	6	6	11	13	14	14	12	9	7	5
Rainfall - mm	203	162	127	133	94	125	160	154	190	214	181	236

Clacton-on-Sea	Jan	Feb	Mar	Apr	May	Jun	Jul	Aug	Sep	Oct	Nov	Dec
Temperature - °C	4	4	6	8	12	15	17	17	15	12	7	5
Rainfall - mm	49	31	43	40	40	45	43	43	48	48	55	50

Plymouth	Jan	Feb	Mar	Apr	May	Jun	Jul	Aug	Sep	Oct	Nov	Dec
Temperature - °C	6	6	7	9	12	15	16	16	15	12	9	7
Rainfall - mm	99	74	69	53	63	53	70	77	78	91	113	110

Temperature: January

The southwest is the warmest due to the effects of the sea. The coldest areas are the uplands and the mountains in the north.

Average temperature

- over 6 °C
- 4–6 °C
- 2–4 °C
- 0–2 °C
- below 0 °C

● Location of places on climate graphs

Scale 1 : 10 000 000

Temperature: July

Warmest are the south facing coasts and the eastern lowlands. Higher land is generally cooler.

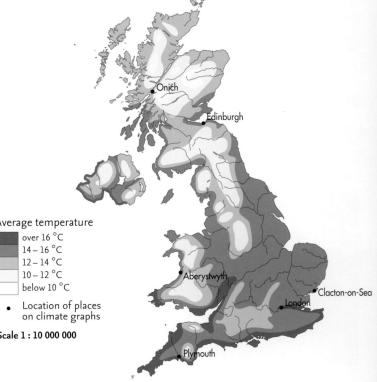

Average temperature

- over 16 °C
- 14–16 °C
- 12–14 °C
- 10–12 °C
- below 10 °C

● Location of places on climate graphs

Scale 1 : 10 000 000

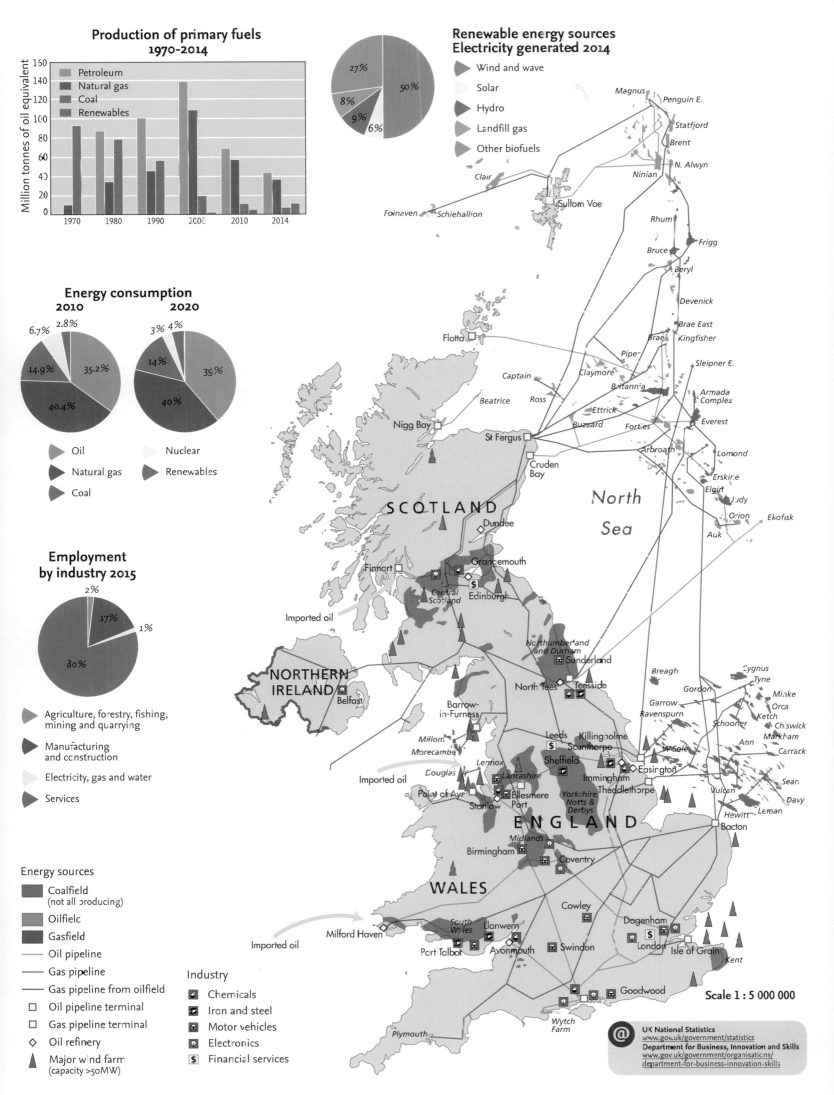

Production of primary fuels 1970-2014

Million tonnes of oil equivalent

- Petroleum
- Natural gas
- Coal
- Renewables

1970 1980 1990 2000 2010 2014

Renewable energy sources Electricity generated 2014

50%
27%
8%
9%
6%

- Wind and wave
- Solar
- Hydro
- Landfill gas
- Other biofuels

Energy consumption

2010
- 2.8%
- 6.7%
- 35.2%
- 14.9%
- 40.4%

2020
- 4%
- 3%
- 39%
- 14%
- 40%

- Oil
- Natural gas
- Coal
- Nuclear
- Renewables

Employment by industry 2015

- 2%
- 17%
- 1%
- 80%

- Agriculture, forestry, fishing, mining and quarrying
- Manufacturing and construction
- Electricity, gas and water
- Services

Energy sources

- Coalfield (not all producing)
- Oilfield
- Gasfield
- Oil pipeline
- Gas pipeline
- Gas pipeline from oilfield
- □ Oil pipeline terminal
- □ Gas pipeline terminal
- ◇ Oil refinery
- ▲ Major wind farm (capacity >50MW)

Industry

- Chemicals
- Iron and steel
- Motor vehicles
- Electronics
- $ Financial services

Scale 1 : 5 000 000

UK National Statistics
www.gov.uk/government/statistics
Department for Business, Innovation and Skills
www.gov.uk/government/organisations/
department-for-business-innovation-skills

SCOTLAND
NORTHERN IRELAND
ENGLAND
WALES
North Sea

Magnus, Penguin E., Statfjord, Brent, N. Alwyn, Ninian, Clair, Foinaven, Schiehallion, Sullom Voe, Rhum, Frigg, Bruce, Beryl, Devenick, Brae East, Kingfisher, Brae, Piper, Claymore, Britannia, Armada Complex, Everest, Flotta, Captain, Ross, Beatrice, Buzzard, Ettrick, Forties, Arbroath, Lomond, Erskine, Elgin, Judy, Orion, Ekofisk, Auk, Nigg Bay, St Fergus, Cruden Bay, Dundee, Finnart, Grangemouth, Central Scotland, Edinburgh, Imported oil, Northumberland and Durham, Sunderland, North Tees, Teesside, Breagh, Cygnus, Tyne, Gordon, Minke, Orca, Garrow, Ravenspurn, Ketch, Schooner, Chiswick, Markham, Ann, Carrack, Barrow-in-Furness, Millom, Morecambe, Leeds, Killingholme, Scunthorpe, Sheffield, Immingham, Theddlethorpe, Easington, W. Sole, Sean, Belfast, Lennox, Lancashire, Yorkshire Notts & Derbys, Vulcan, Davy, Douglas, Point of Ayr, Ellesmere Port, Stanlow, Hewitt, Leman, Midlands, Bacton, Birmingham, Coventry, Cowley, Dagenham, South Wales, Llanwern, Swindon, London, Milford Haven, Port Talbot, Avonmouth, Isle of Grain, Kent, Goodwood, Imported oil, Wytch Farm, Plymouth

Country boundary
Internal boundary
Road
Railway
Ferry route
✈ Airport
■ Capital city
■ Regional capital
◉ Large town or city
○ Other town or city

Scale 1 : 4 000 000

Shetland Islands

Lerwick

Kirkwall
Aberdeen

ATLANTIC OCEAN

North Sea

Stornoway
Tarbert
Lochmaddy
Uig
Portree
Lochboisdale
Mallaig
Fort William
Tobermory
Oban
Ullapool
Inverness
Stromness
Kirkwall
Thurso
Wick
Lerwick

SCOTLAND

Aberdeen
Perth
Dundee
Stirling
M90
M9
Glasgow M8 **Edinburgh**
Ardrossan
Troon
Ayr
Brodick
Campbeltown
M74
Berwick-upon-Tweed

Coleraine
Londonderry (Derry)
M2
Larne
Donegal
NORTHERN IRELAND
Enniskillen
M1
Belfast
Lisburn
Newry
Ballina
Sligo
Westport
Dundalk
Drogheda
M3
Douglas
Cairnryan
Stranraer
Dumfries
A74 (M)
Carlisle
Workington
Morpeth
Newcastle upon Tyne
Sunderland
Durham
A1 (M)
Darlington
Middlesbrough
Scarborough

Galway
M6
M18
M50
Dublin
Dún Laoghaire
M11
Wicklow
M8
M9
M7
M11
Limerick
M20
Tralee
M8
Waterford
Cork
Wexford
Rosslare

Holyhead
Heysham
Lancaster
Harrogate
York
Kingston upon Hull
Blackpool
Bradford
Leeds
M62
Preston
Huddersfield
Doncaster
Grimsby
Bolton
Manchester
Stockport
Sheffield
Lincoln
Liverpool
Chester
Crewe
Stoke-on-Trent
Derby
Nottingham
Caernarfon

Irish Sea

Fishguard
Pembroke
Swansea
Newport
Bridgend
Cardiff
Aberystwyth
WALES
Hereford
Gloucester
Shrewsbury
Telford
ENGLAND
Wolverhampton
Birmingham
Warwick
Coventry
M5
M6
Northampton
Peterborough
King's Lynn
Norwich
Great Yarmouth
Cambridge
Ipswich
Felixstowe
Harwich
M1
M11
Oxford
M40
Luton
Watford
Swindon
Slough
M25
London
Reading
M4
Bath
Bristol
Ramsgate
Croydon
M20
M2
Ashford
Dover
Folkestone
Southend-on-Sea
Crawley
Brighton
Hastings
Eastbourne
Newhaven
Boulogne-sur-Mer
Salisbury
Taunton
Southampton
Portsmouth
Poole
Bournemouth
M5
Exeter
Weymouth
Torquay
Plymouth
Penzance

IRELAND

English Channel

Cherbourg, Roscoff
Roscoff Santander
Gijón-Xixón, Santander
Bilbao, Channel Islands, St Malo
Channel Islands; St Malo
Cherbourg
Le Havre
Caen
Rouen
Dieppe
FRANCE

Amsterdam
Rotterdam Zeebrugge
Hoek van Holland
Ostend
Dunkerque
Calais

UK National Statistics
www.gov.uk/government/statistics
Department for Transport
www.gov.uk/government/organisations/department-for-transport

Population density

The greatest concentration of population in the United Kingdom is found in the areas immediately surrounding London where the number of persons per square kilometre is more than 500 times greater than in the Scottish Highlands. The total population of England is greater than the sum of the populations of Scotland, Wales and Northern Ireland.

Persons per sq km
- over 150
- 10 – 150
- 0 – 10

Cities and towns
- over 5 000 000
- 1 000 000 – 5 000 000
- 500 000 – 1 000 000
- 100 000 – 500 000
- 20 000 – 100 000

Scale 1 : 5 000 000

Population by country
2014

- Eng and
- Scotland
- Wales
- Northern Ireland

5% 3%
8%
84%

2014 UK total 64 596 000

Increase in population
1901-2031

Dotted line indicates projected population

Population in millions

1901 1911 1921 1931 1951 1961 1981 2001 2011 2021 2031

- United Kingdom
- England
- Scotland
- Wales
- Northern Ireland

Population structure
2015

Percentage

Age group
- over 74
- 60 – 74
- 45 – 59
- 30 – 44
- 15 – 29
- 0 – 14

Males Females

@ UK National Statistics
www.gov.uk/government/statistics
The Census in England and Wales
www.statistics.gov.uk/census
The Census in Scotland
www.gro-scotland.gov.uk/statistics-and-data/census

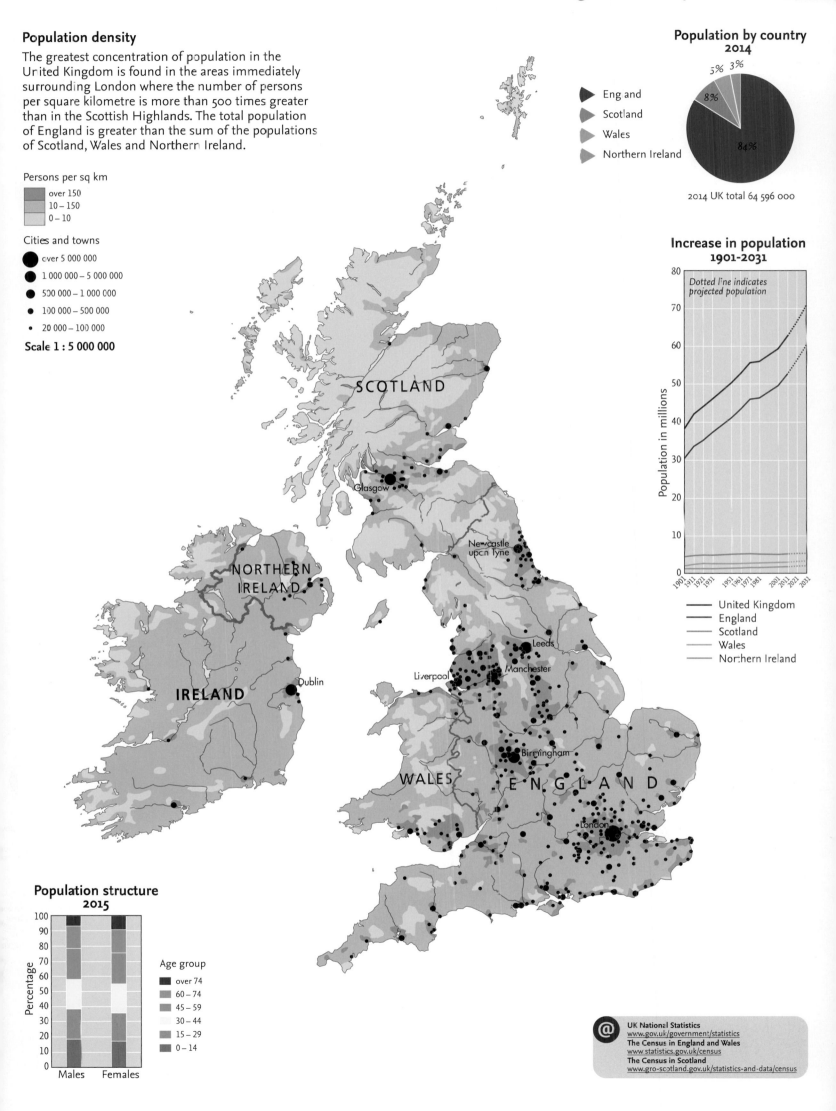

SCOTLAND

NORTHERN IRELAND

IRELAND

Dublin

Glasgow

Newcastle upon Tyne

Leeds

Liverpool Manchester

Birmingham

WALES ENGLAND

London

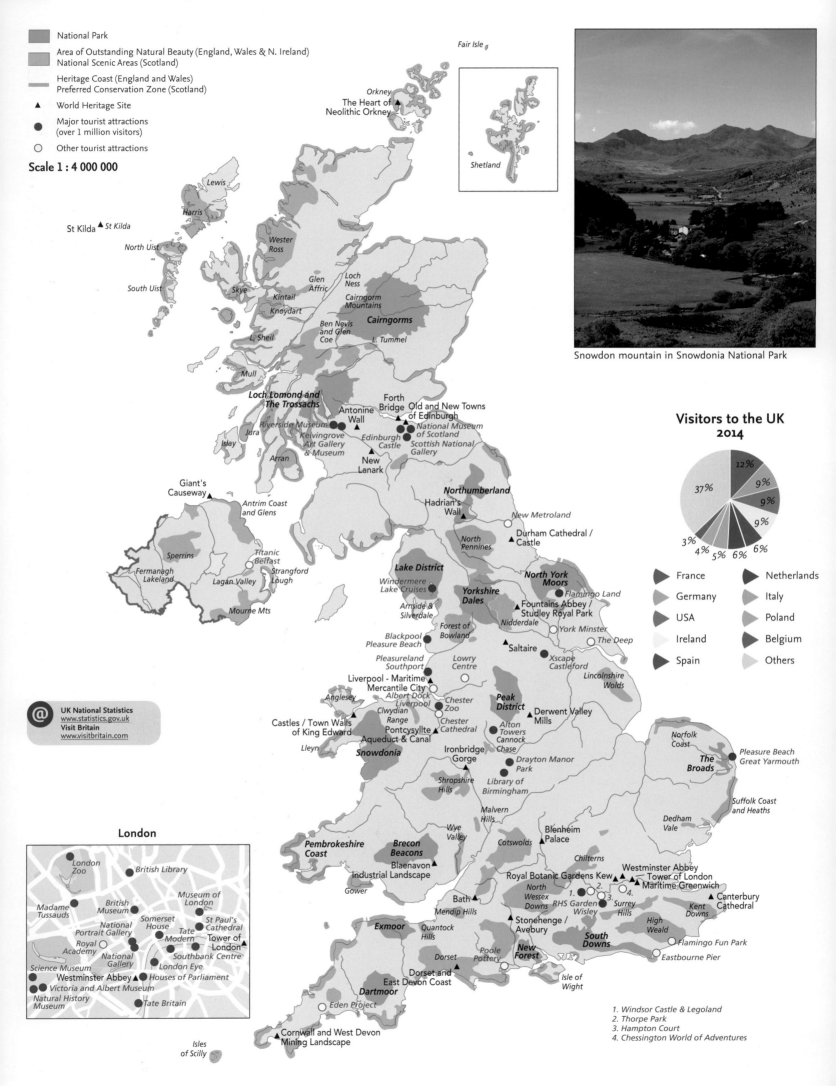

National Park

Area of Outstanding Natural Beauty (England, Wales & N. Ireland)
National Scenic Areas (Scotland)

Heritage Coast (England and Wales)
Preferred Conservation Zone (Scotland)

▲ World Heritage Site

● Major tourist attractions
(over 1 million visitors)

○ Other tourist attractions

Scale 1 : 4 000 000

Snowdon mountain in Snowdonia National Park

Visitors to the UK 2014

37%
12%
9%
9%
9%
6%
6%
5%
4%
3%

◤ France
◤ Germany
◤ USA
◤ Ireland
◤ Spain
◤ Netherlands
◤ Italy
◤ Poland
◤ Belgium
◤ Others

UK National Statistics
www.statistics.gov.uk
Visit Britain
www.visitbritain.com

London

London Zoo
British Library
Madame Tussauds
British Museum
Museum of London
National Portrait Gallery
Somerset House
Tate Modern
St Paul's Cathedral
Royal Academy
National Gallery
Tower of London
Science Museum
Southbank Centre
London Eye
Westminster Abbey ▲
Houses of Parliament
Natural History Museum
Victoria and Albert Museum
Tate Britain

Fair Isle
Orkney
The Heart of Neolithic Orkney ▲
Shetland
Lewis
Harris
St Kilda ▲ St Kilda
North Uist
Wester Ross
South Uist
Skye
Glen Affric
Loch Ness
Kintail
Knoydart
Cairngorm Mountains
Ben Nevis and Glen Coe
L. Sheil
Cairngorms
L. Tummel
Mull
Jura
Islay
Arran
Loch Lomond and The Trossachs
Riverside Museum
Antonine Wall
Kelvingrove Art Gallery & Museum
Forth Bridge
Old and New Towns of Edinburgh
National Museum of Scotland
Edinburgh Castle
Scottish National Gallery
New Lanark
Giant's Causeway ▲
Antrim Coast and Glens
Titanic Belfast
Sperrins
Strangford Lough
Fermanagh Lakeland
Lagan Valley
Mourne Mts
Northumberland
Hadrian's Wall
New Metroland
North Pennines
Durham Cathedral / Castle
Lake District
Windermere Lake Cruises
North York Moors
Flamingo Land
Yorkshire Dales
Arnside & Silverdale
Fountains Abbey / Studley Royal Park
Nidderdale
York Minster
The Deep
Forest of Bowland
Blackpool Pleasure Beach
Saltaire
Xscape Castleford
Pleasureland Southport
Lowry Centre
Lincolnshire Wolds
Liverpool - Maritime Mercantile City
Albert Dock
Liverpool
Anglesey
Chester Zoo
Chester Cathedral
Peak District
Derwent Valley Mills
Clwydian Range
Alton Towers
Cannock Chase
Norfolk Coast
Castles / Town Walls of King Edward
Pontcysyllte Aqueduct & Canal
Ironbridge Gorge
Drayton Manor Park
The Broads
Pleasure Beach Great Yarmouth
Lleyn
Snowdonia
Shropshire Hills
Library of Birmingham
Suffolk Coast and Heaths
Malvern Hills
Dedham Vale
Wye Valley
Blenheim Palace
Pembrokeshire Coast
Brecon Beacons
Cotswolds
Chilterns
Norfolk Coast
Blaenavon Industrial Landscape
Gower
Royal Botanic Gardens Kew
Westminster Abbey
Tower of London
Maritime Greenwich
Bath
North Wessex Downs
1. 2. 3. 4.
Canterbury Cathedral
Kent Downs
Mendip Hills
RHS Garden Wisley
Surrey Hills
High Weald
Exmoor
Quantock Hills
Stonehenge / Avebury
South Downs
Flamingo Fun Park
Dorset
Poole Pottery
New Forest
Eastbourne Pier
Dorset and East Devon Coast
Isle of Wight
Dartmoor
Eden Project
Cornwall and West Devon Mining Landscape
Isles of Scilly

1. Windsor Castle & Legoland
2. Thorpe Park
3. Hampton Court
4. Chessington World of Adventures

The UK has played a key role in the development of international sports including: football, rugby, golf, tennis, badminton, squash, rounders, snooker, hockey, boxing, billiards, curling, sailing and motor racing. The hosting of events, such as the Commonwealth and Olympic Games, can inspire young people to participate in either team or individual sporting activities. Swimming, cycling and athletics tend to have the highest active participation.

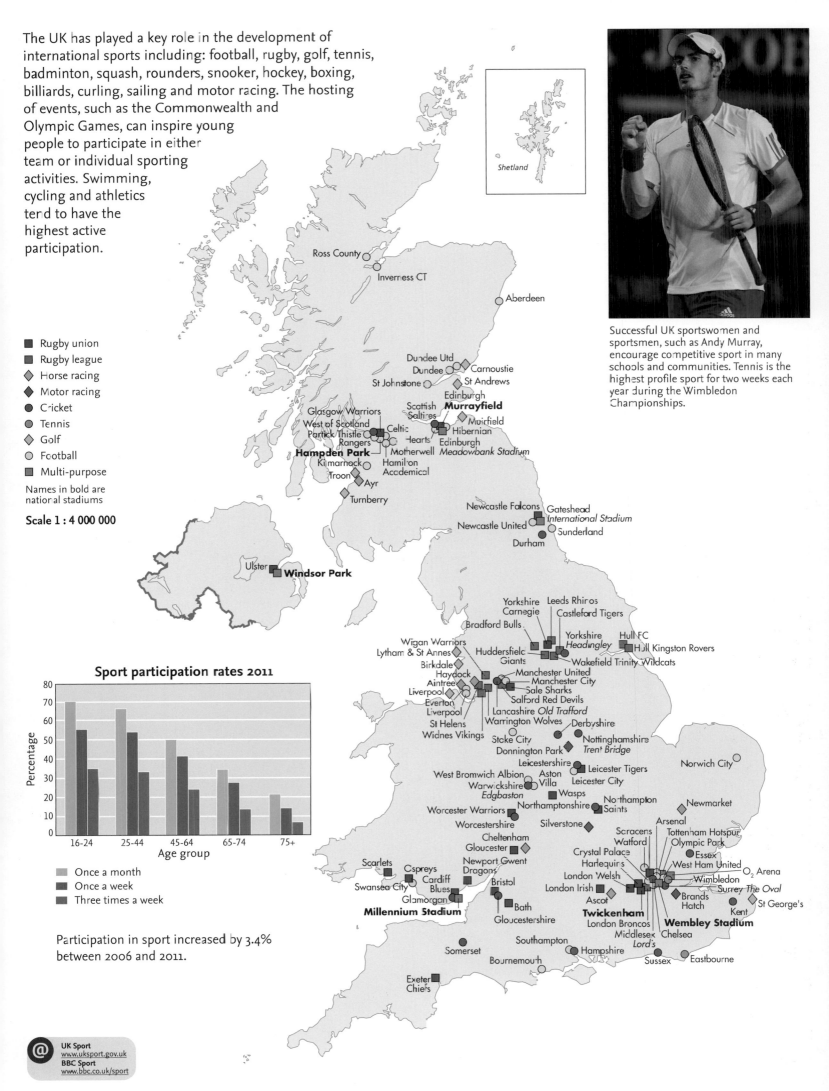

Successful UK sportswomen and sportsmen, such as Andy Murray, encourage competitive sport in many schools and communities. Tennis is the highest profile sport for two weeks each year during the Wimbledon Championships.

Shetland

Legend

- ■ Rugby union
- ■ Rugby league
- ◆ Horse racing
- ◆ Motor racing
- ● Cricket
- ● Tennis
- ◆ Golf
- ○ Football
- ■ Multi-purpose

Names in bold are national stadiums

Scale 1 : 4 000 000

Sport participation rates 2011

Percentage (y-axis: 0, 10, 20, 30, 40, 50, 60, 70, 80)

Age group (x-axis: 16–24, 25–44, 45–64, 65–74, 75+)

- Once a month
- Once a week
- Three times a week

Participation in sport increased by 3.4% between 2006 and 2011.

UK Sport
www.uksport.gov.uk
BBC Sport
www.bbc.co.uk/sport

Map labels:

Ross County, Inverness CT, Aberdeen, Dundee Utd, Dundee, Carnoustie, St Johnstone, St Andrews, Edinburgh, Scottish Saltires, **Murrayfield**, Glasgow Warriors, West of Scotland, Partick Thistle, Rangers, Celtic, Hearts, Muirfield, Hibernian, Edinburgh *Meadowbank Stadium*, **Hampden Park**, Kilmarnock, Motherwell, Hamilton Academical, Troon, Ayr, Turnberry

Ulster, **Windsor Park**

Newcastle Falcons, Gateshead *International Stadium*, Newcastle United, Sunderland, Durham

Yorkshire Carnegie, Leeds Rhinos, Castleford Tigers, Bradford Bulls, Wigan Warriors, Yorkshire *Headingley*, Hull FC, Hull Kingston Rovers, Lytham & St Annes, Huddersfield Giants, Wakefield Trinity Wildcats, Birkdale, Haydock, Manchester United, Manchester City, Aintree, Sale Sharks, Liverpool, Salford Red Devils, Everton, Lancashire *Old Trafford*, Liverpool, Warrington Wolves, Derbyshire, St Helens, Widnes Vikings, Stoke City, Nottinghamshire *Trent Bridge*, Donnington Park, Leicestershire, Leicester Tigers, Norwich City, West Bromwich Albion, Aston Villa, Leicester City, Warwickshire *Edgbaston*, Wasps, Northampton Saints, Newmarket, Worcester Warriors, Northamptonshire, Silverstone, Arsenal, Worcestershire, Silverstone, Tottenham Hotspur, Cheltenham, Saracens, Watford, Olympic Park, Essex, Gloucester, Crystal Palace, West Ham United, Newport Gwent Dragons, Harlequins, London Welsh, O₂ Arena, Scarlets, Ospreys, Cardiff Blues, Bristol, London Irish, Wimbledon, Swansea City, Glamorgan, Ascot, Brands Hatch, Surrey *The Oval*, **Millennium Stadium**, Bath, Gloucestershire, **Twickenham**, London Broncos, Middlesex *Lord's*, Chelsea, **Wembley Stadium**, Kent, St George's, Somerset, Southampton, Hampshire, Eastbourne, Bournemouth, Sussex, Exeter Chiefs

North Sea

Irish Sea

North Channel

SCOTLAND

ENGLAND

NORTHERN IRELAND

IRELAND

Firth of Tay
Firth of Forth
Firth of Clyde
Solway Firth
Southern Uplands
Cheviot Hills
Pennines
Lake District
North York Moors
High Peak
Antrim Hills
Mourne Mts
Isle of Man
Anglesey

Edinburgh
Glasgow
Newcastle upon Tyne
Leeds
Manchester
Liverpool
Belfast

Oban
Ullapool
Tobermory
Mull
Ben More 966
Colonsay
Islay
Port Askaig
Port Ellen
Jura
Inveraray
Lochgilphead
Crianlarich
Ben Lomond 974
Callander
Crieff
Pitlochry
Blairgowrie
Dundee
Forfar
Arbroath
St Andrews
Perth
Ochil Hills
Kinross
Dunfermline
Glenrothes
Kirkcaldy
Loch Tay
Tay
Loch Lomond
Dumbarton
Clydebank
Paisley
Greenock
Rothesay
Brodick
Arran
Bute
Campbeltown
Mull of Kintyre
East Kilbride
Hamilton
Motherwell
Falkirk
Stirling
Livingston
Dalkeith
Peebles
Biggar
Moffat
Lanark
Ayr
Prestwick
Irvine
Kilmarnock
Clyde
Girvan
Merrick 843
Newton Stewart
Stranraer
Whithorn
Castle Douglas
Dumfries
Sanquhar
Nith
Lockerbie
Hawick
Ettrick Water
Teviot
Jedburgh
Galashiels
Coldstream
Tweed
Berwick-upon-Tweed
Dunbar

Loch Linnhe

Loch Fyne
Kintyre

Downpatrick
Downpatrick
Newcastle
Slieve Donard 852
Bangor
Newtownabbey
Larne
Lisburn
Antrim
Lough Neagh
Skerries
Dún Laoghaire
Bray
Wicklow
Wicklow Mts
Holyhead
Caernarfon Bay
Caernarfon
Bangor
Colwyn Bay
Rhyl
Snowdon 1085
Ffestiniog
Clwyd
Dee
Mold
Wrexham
Chester
Ellesmere Port
Birkenhead
Crewe
Stoke-on-Trent
Derby
Macclesfield
Stockport
Oldham
Rochdale
Bolton
Blackburn
Burnley
Wigan
St Helens
Warrington
Mersey
Southport
Formby
Blackpool
Preston
Lancaster
Morecambe
Morecambe Bay
Lune
Kendal
Windermere
Barrow-in-Furness
Whitehaven
Workington
Scafell Pike 977
Penrith
Carlisle
Longtown
Ribble
Skipton
Bradford
Halifax
Huddersfield
Wakefield
Rotherham
Sheffield
Chesterfield
Mansfield
Nottingham
Barnsley
Doncaster
York
Selby
Goole
Harrogate
Ripon
Ure
Nidd
Ouse
Northallerton
Swale
Darlington
Stockton-on-Tees
Middlesbrough
Hartlepool
Tees
Bishop Auckland
Durham
Wear
Sunderland
South Shields
Morpeth
Alnwick
Tyne
Whitby
Scarborough
Flamborough Head
Bridlington
Beverley
Kingston upon Hull
Humber
Scunthorpe
Goole
Derwent
Grimsby
Cleethorpes
Spurn Head
Louth
Lincoln
Witham
Boston
Grantham
Trent
The Wash
Skegness
Cromer
Norfolk
Douglas

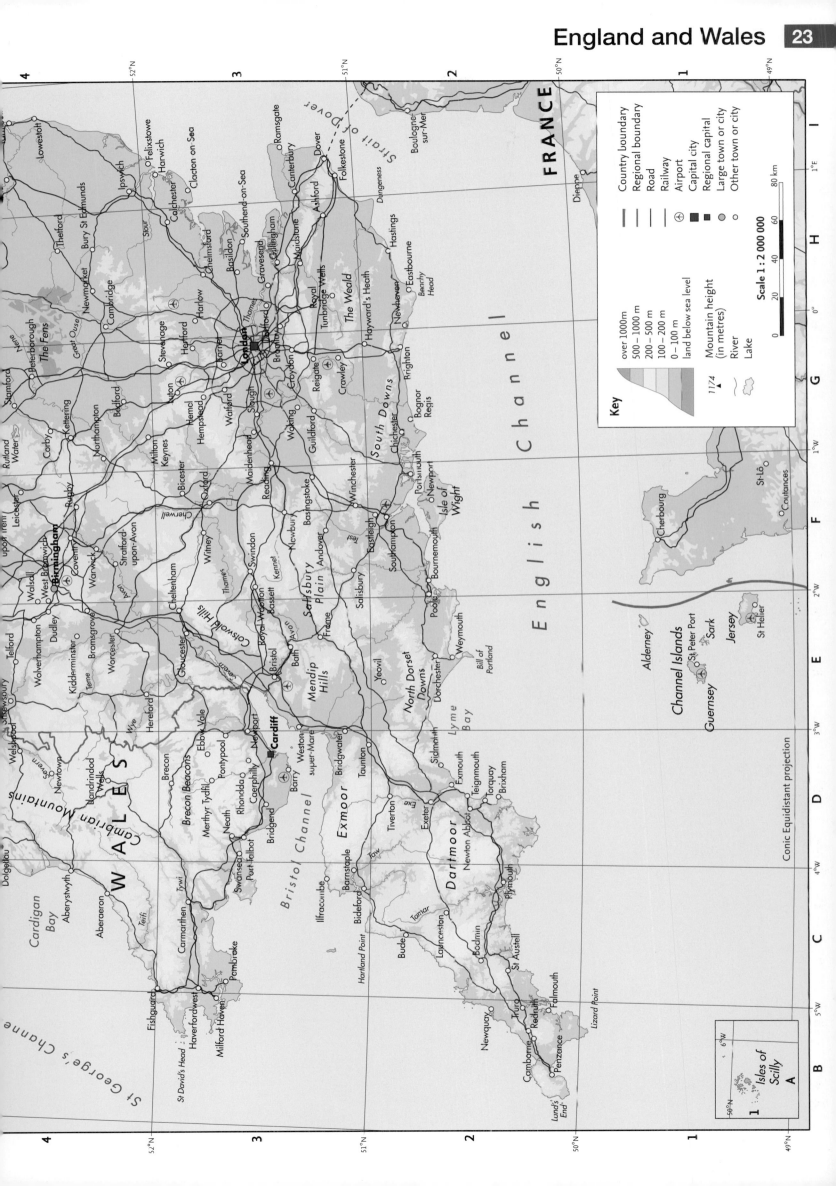

Key

		Country boundary
		Regional boundary
		Road
		Railway
✈		Airport
■		Capital city
■		Regional capital
●		Large town or city
○		Other town or city

Scale 1 : 2 000 000

| over 1000 m |
| 500 – 1000 m |
| 200 – 500 m |
| 100 – 200 m |
| 0 – 100 m |
| land below sea level |

1 174 ▲ Mountain height (in metres)

～ River

Lake

0   20   40   60   80 km

FRANCE

England and Wales

Conic Equidistant projection

Conic Equidistant projection

ATLANTIC OCEAN

SCOTLAND

Fort Askaig
Jura
Islay
Port Ellen
Rothesay
Bute
Arran
Brodick
Irvine
Prestwick
Ayr
Campbeltown
Mull of Kintyre
Girvan
Stranraer
Firth of Clyde
North Channel
Antrim Hills

Malin Head
Bloody Foreland
Errigal 752
Lough Foyle
Portrush
Coleraine
Londonderry (Derry)
Letterkenny
Blue Stack 676
Strabane
Ballymena
Antrim
Larne
Newtownabbey
Bangor
Belfast
Donegal
Omagh
Dungannon
Lisburn
Downpatrick
Donegal Bay
Lower Lough Erne
Enniskillen
Upper Lough Erne
Monaghan
Lough Neagh
Armagh
Newry
Newcastle
Mourne Mts
Slieve Donard 852

NORTHERN IRELAND

Erris Head
Belmullet
Ballina
Lough Conn
Sligo
Carrick-on-Shannon
Cavan
Dundalk
Dundalk Bay
Achill Island
Castlebar
Lough Allen
Westport
Claremorris
Longford
Navan
Drogheda
Skerries
Lough Mask
Roscommon
Lough Ree
Mullingar
Boyne
Irish Sea
Connemara
Lough Corrib
Athlone
Dublin
Galway
Tullamore
Liffey
Dún Laoghaire
Naas
Bray
Galway Bay
Lough Derg
Shannon
Portlaoise
Wicklow Mts
Wicklow
Wicklow Head
Aran Islands
Roscrea
Ennis
Nenagh
Barrow
Nore
Carlow
Arklow
Kilkee
Kilrush
Limerick
Thurles
Kilkenny
Enniscorthy
Tipperary
Suir
New Ross
Tralee
Clonmel
Cahir
Carrick-on-Suir
Wexford
Rosslare
Dingle
Mallow
Blackwater
Fermoy
Knockmealdown Mts
Dungarvan
Waterford
Youghal
WALES
Dingle Bay
Killarney
Carrantuohill 1041
Boggeragh Mts
Lee
Cork
Cobh
Old Head of Kinsale
Sneem
Bantry
Skibbereen
Fishguard
Mizen Head
Cape Clear
St George's Channel

IRELAND

Celtic Sea

Key

over 1000m	Country boundary
500 – 1000 m	Regional boundary
200 – 500 m	Road
100 – 200 m	Railway
0 – 100 m	⊕ Airport
land below sea level	■ Capital city
	■ Regional capital
▲ 1345 Mountain height (in metres)	⬤ Large town or city
River	○ Other town or city
Lake	

Scale 1 : 2 000 000

0   20   40   60   80 km

Key

over 5000 m
3000 – 5000 m
2000 – 3000 m
1000 – 2000 m
500 – 1000 m
200 – 500 m
0 – 200 m
land below sea level

Ice cap

▲ 5642 Mountain height (in metres)

Scale 1 : 25 000 000

0   250   500   750   1000 km

Facts about Europe Relief

Area
9 908 599 sq km

Highest peak
Mt Elbrus 5642 m

Lowest point
Caspian Sea -28 m

Longest river
Volga 3688 km

Largest lake
Caspian Sea 371 000 sq km

Conic Equidistant projection

Climate zones

Europe's climate varies from temperate, wet conditions in the west, to a drier continental climate in the east. The far north experiences sub-arctic conditions in contrast to the warm, dry Mediterranean climate of the south.

Scale 1 : 45 000 000

Semi-arid	Temperate	Mountain
Mediterranean	Continental cool summer	Sub-arctic
Wet subtropical	Continental warm summer	Tundra

Climate graphs

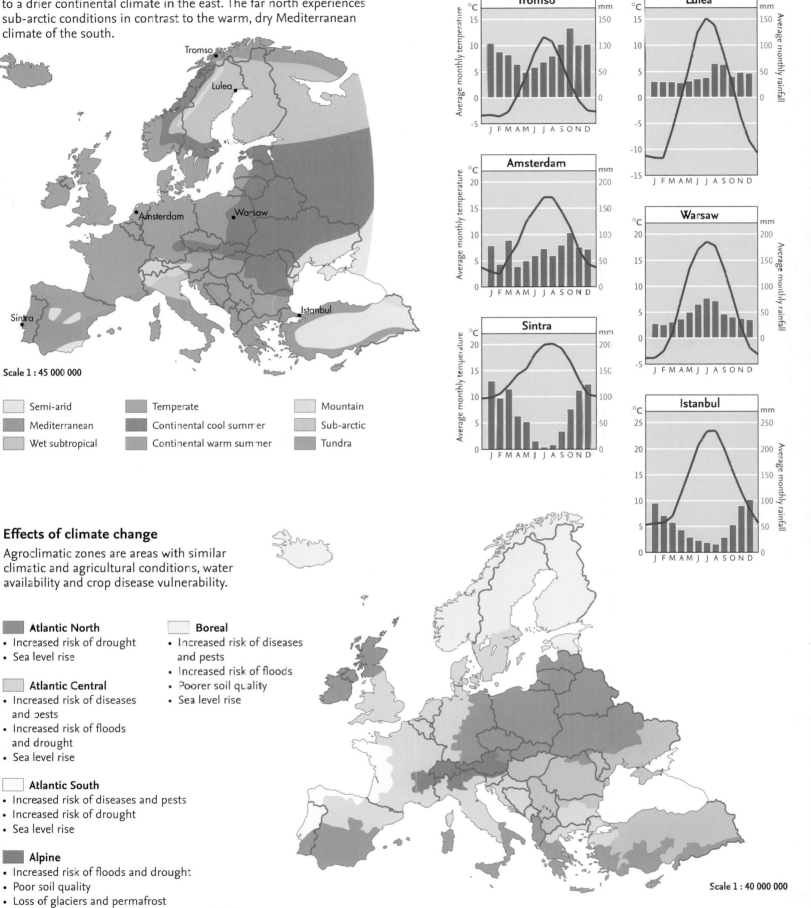

Effects of climate change

Agroclimatic zones are areas with similar climatic and agricultural conditions, water availability and crop disease vulnerability.

Atlantic North
• Increased risk of drought
• Sea level rise

Atlantic Central
• Increased risk of diseases and pests
• Increased risk of floods and drought
• Sea level rise

Atlantic South
• Increased risk of diseases and pests
• Increased risk of drought
• Sea level rise

Alpine
• Increased risk of floods and drought
• Poor soil quality
• Loss of glaciers and permafrost

Boreal
• Increased risk of diseases and pests
• Increased risk of floods
• Poorer soil quality
• Sea level rise

Scale 1 : 40 000 000

Mediterranean North
• Increased risk of diseases and pests
• Increased risk of drought
• Increased need for irrigation
• Poor soil quality
• Sea level rise

Mediterranean South
• Increased risk of diseases and pests
• Decline in crop quality
• Increased risk of drought
• Increased need for irrigation
• Poor soil quality
• Sea level rise

Continental North
• Increased risk of diseases and pests
• Increased risk of floods and drought
• Sea level rise

Continental South
• Increased risk of diseases and pests
• Increased risk of drought
• Increased need for irrigation
• Poor soil quality

Key

— Country boundary
--- Disputed boundary
■ Capital city
○ Important city

Scale 1 : 25 000 000

0   250   500   750   1000 km

Country abbreviations

A. ANDORRA
BEL. BELGIUM
B.H. BOSNIA AND HERZEGOVINA
K. KOSOVO
L. LIECHTENSTEIN
LUX. LUXEMBOURG
MAC. MACEDONIA (FYROM)
MO. MONTENEGRO
NETH. NETHERLANDS
SL. SLOVENIA
SW. SWITZERLAND

Facts about Europe countries (excluding Russia)

Population
594 823 000

Largest city
Istanbul 12 459 000

Largest country
Ukraine 603 700 sq km

Country with most people
Germany 80 689 000

Conic Equidistant projection

European Union members

The European Union (EU) was created in 1957 by the Treaty of Rome. The original members of the then European Economic Community (EEC) were Belgium, France, West Germany, Italy, Luxembourg and the Netherlands. Since 1957 the EU has grown and now has 28 member states. The total population of the EU is now over 500 million.

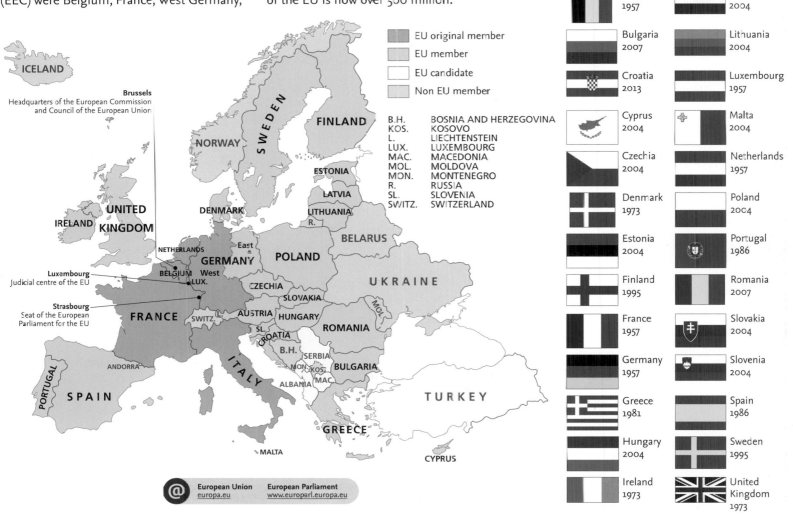

- EU original member
- EU member
- EU candidate
- Non EU member

B.H.	BOSNIA AND HERZEGOVINA
KOS.	KOSOVO
L.	LIECHTENSTEIN
LUX.	LUXEMBOURG
MAC.	MACEDONIA
MOL.	MOLDOVA
MON.	MONTENEGRO
R.	RUSSIA
SL.	SLOVENIA
SWITZ.	SWITZERLAND

Brussels
Headquarters of the European Commission and Council of the European Union

Luxembourg
Judicial centre of the EU

Strasbourg
Seat of the European Parliament for the EU

@ European Union
europa.eu

European Parliament
www.europarl.europa.eu

Austria 1995	Italy 1957
Belgium 1957	Latvia 2004
Bulgaria 2007	Lithuania 2004
Croatia 2013	Luxembourg 1957
Cyprus 2004	Malta 2004
Czechia 2004	Netherlands 1957
Denmark 1973	Poland 2004
Estonia 2004	Portugal 1986
Finland 1995	Romania 2007
France 1957	Slovakia 2004
Germany 1957	Slovenia 2004
Greece 1981	Spain 1986
Hungary 2004	Sweden 1995
Ireland 1973	United Kingdom 1973

EU migration

Europeans have a long history of migration and although many emigrate to outside of Europe there is an increase in movement within the EU zone. EU citizens can travel, work and live in other member states with few restrictions. Most states have abolished passport and customs checks between members.

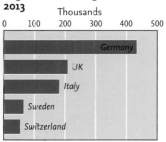

Highest net immigration
2013
Thousands
0 100 200 300 400 500

- Germany
- UK
- Italy
- Sweden
- Switzerland

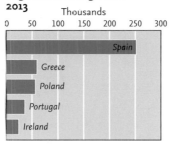

Highest net emigration
2013
Thousands
0 50 100 150 200 250 300

- Spain
- Greece
- Poland
- Portugal
- Ireland

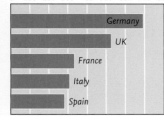

Highest number of immigrants
2013
Thousands
0 100 200 300 400 500 600 700 800

- Germany
- UK
- France
- Italy
- Spain

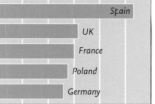

Highest number of emigrants
2013
Thousands
0 100 200 300 400 500 600

- Spain
- UK
- France
- Poland
- Germany

Euro countries

In 2002 **euro (€)** bank notes and coins were introduced and 19 member states (the Eurozone) now use the **euro** as their official currency. There are 7 denominations of notes and 8 coins. It is likely that more members will adopt the **euro** in the future.

- Eurozone
- Non Eurozone
- Non EU member

A. ANDORRA
KOS. KOSOVO
L. LIECHTENSTEIN
LUX. LUXEMBOURG
M. MONACO
MON. MONTENEGRO
NETH. NETHERLANDS
S.M. SAN MARINO

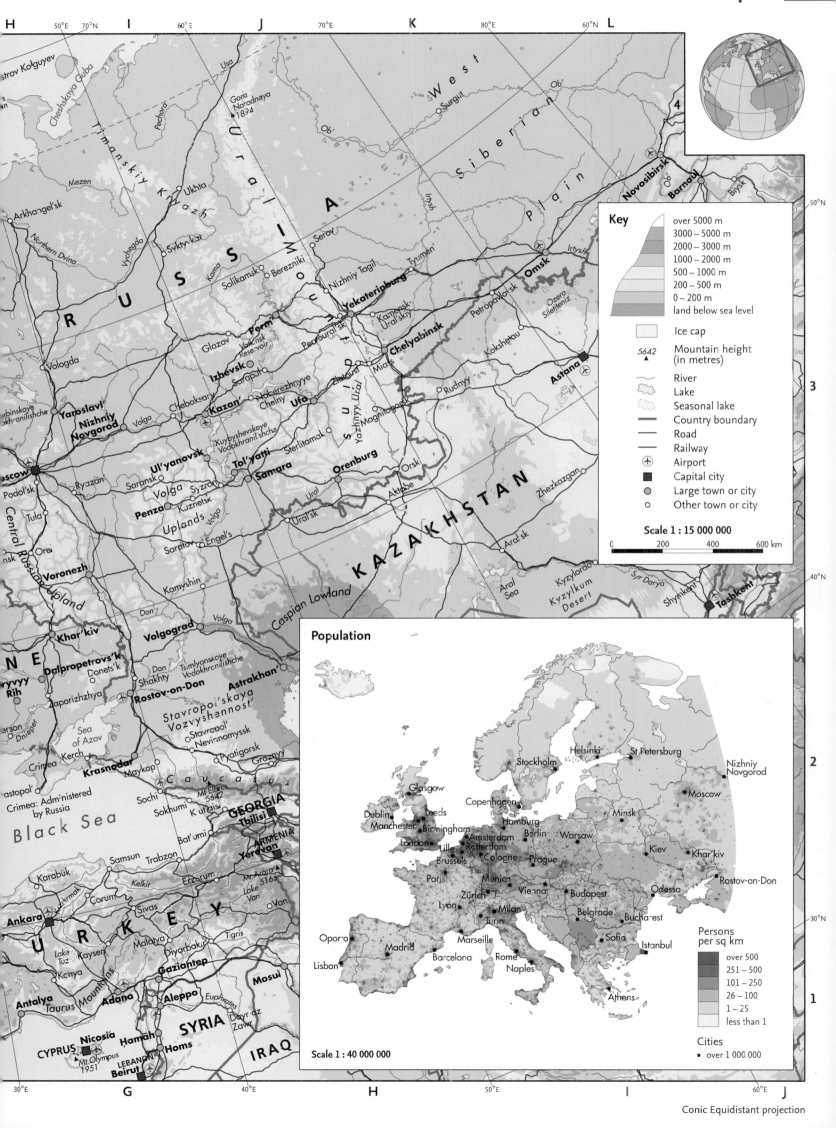

Conic Equidistant projection

Facts about Italy

Landscape
Area: 301 245 sq km
Highest point: Mont Blanc 4810 m

Population
Total: 59 798 000
Density: 199 persons per sq km

Settlement
% Urban population: 70
Main towns: Rome, Milan, Naples, Turin

Land use
Main crops: Sugar beets, corn, grapes
Main industries: Machinery, metal products, chemicals, food

Development indicators
Life expectancy: male 80, female 85
GNI per capita: US$ 34 280
Primary school enrolment ratio: 96
% Access to safe water: 100

Key

over 5000 m
3000 – 5000 m
2000 – 3000 m
1000 – 2000 m
500 – 1000 m
200 – 500 m
0 – 200 m
land below sea level
4810 ▲ Mountain height (in metres)
Ice cap

〜 River
Lake
Country boundary
Road
Railway
Ferry
⊕ Airport
■ Capital city
● Large town or city
○ Other town or city

Scale 1 : 5 250 000
0 50 100 150 200 km

Lambert Conformal Conic projection

Regional differences

Italy is divided into three clearly defined physical regions, **North**, **Centre** and **South**. More than 45% of the total population live in the North, less than 20% in Centre and 35% in the South. Economically, significant regional disparities exist between North/Centre and the South, where employment rates are noticeably lower than the national average.

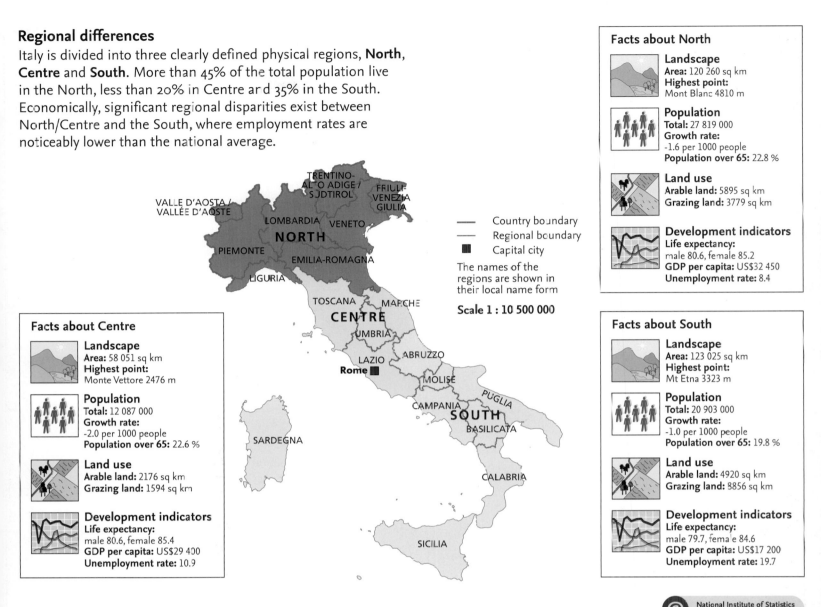

Country boundary
Regional boundary
Capital city

The names of the regions are shown in their local name form

Scale 1 : 10 500 000

Facts about North

Landscape
Area: 120 260 sq km
Highest point:
Mont Blanc 4810 m

Population
Total: 27 819 000
Growth rate:
-1.6 per 1000 people
Population over 65: 22.8 %

Land use
Arable land: 5895 sq km
Grazing land: 3779 sq km

Development indicators
Life expectancy:
male 80.6, female 85.2
GDP per capita: US$32 450
Unemployment rate: 8.4

Facts about Centre

Landscape
Area: 58 051 sq km
Highest point:
Monte Vettore 2476 m

Population
Total: 12 087 000
Growth rate:
-2.0 per 1000 people
Population over 65: 22.6 %

Land use
Arable land: 2176 sq km
Grazing land: 1594 sq km

Development indicators
Life expectancy:
male 80.6, female 85.4
GDP per capita: US$29 400
Unemployment rate: 10.9

Facts about South

Landscape
Area: 123 025 sq km
Highest point:
Mt Etna 3323 m

Population
Total: 20 903 000
Growth rate:
-1.0 per 1000 people
Population over 65: 19.8 %

Land use
Arable land: 4920 sq km
Grazing land: 8856 sq km

Development indicators
Life expectancy:
male 79.7, female 84.6
GDP per capita: US$17 200
Unemployment rate: 19.7

@ National Institute of Statistics
www.istat.it

Earthquakes and volcanoes

Italy lies close to the boundary of the Eurasian Plate with the African Plate and is the only country in mainland Europe where active volcanoes are found. Three of these have erupted in the last hundred years. Mount Etna and Stromboli are continuously active and Vesuvius' last eruption was in 1944.

Volcanic rocks
Principal fault line
△ Volcanoes active in last 100 years
● Major earthquake since 1900

Scale 1 : 10 500 000

Major earthquakes in Italy since 1900

Date	Location	Fatalities	Magnitude*
1905	Capo Vaticano, Calabria	527	7.9
1908	Messina, Sicilia	70 000	7.2
1915	Avezzano, Abruzzo	32 610	7.0
1919	Mugello, Toscana	100	6.3
1920	Garfagnana, Toscana	171	6.4
1930	Irpinia, Campania	1404	6.5
1968	Salaparuta, Sicilia	260	6.5
1976	Gemona del Friuli, Friuli–Venezia Giulia	1000	6.5
1980	Irpinia, Campania	3000	6.5
1997	Annifo, Umbria	11	6.4
2002	Palermo, Sicilia	2	6.0
2002	San Giuliano, Molise	29	5.9
2009	L'Aquila, Abruzzo	295	6.3
2012	Finale Emilia, Emilia-Romagna	7	6.1
2012	Medolla, Emilia-Romagna	20	5.8

* on the Richter scale (see page 50)

National Parks and Protected Areas have been created in Italy to preserve wildlife and natural vegetation. Most of these areas are inland. Along its coastline, Italy has thirty protected coastal areas, including the Cinque Terre Marine Protected Area which became a World Heritage Site in 1997. Pollution from oil spillage and industrial waste remains around the coast for long periods due to the low tidal movements of the Mediterranean Sea.

Manarola, part of the Cinque Terre World Heritage Site

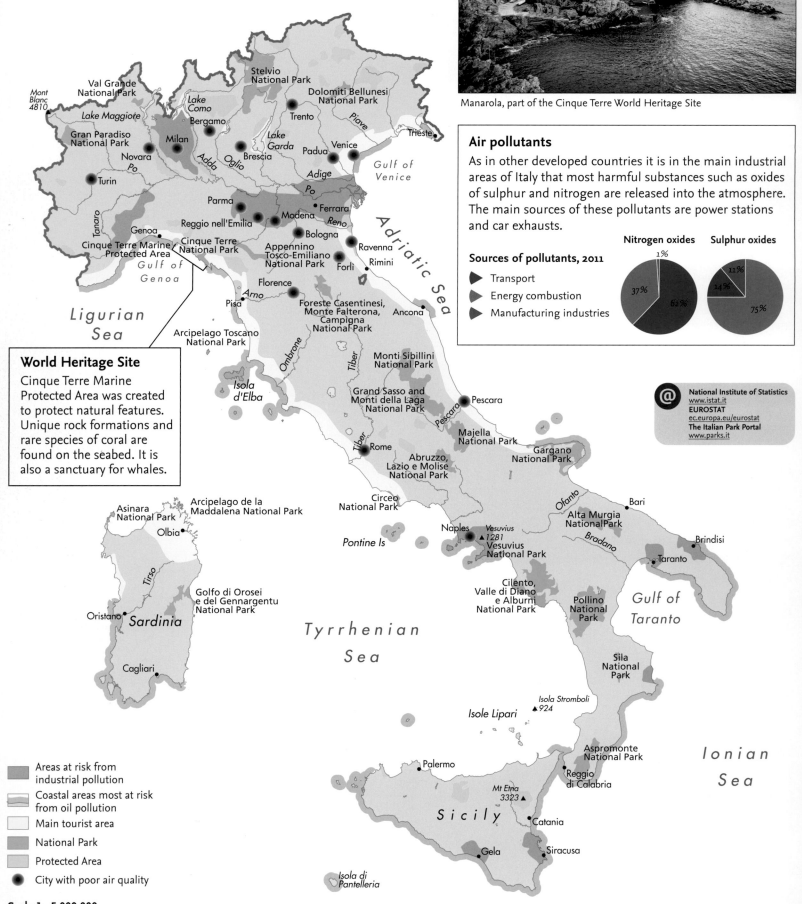

Air pollutants

As in other developed countries it is in the main industrial areas of Italy that most harmful substances such as oxides of sulphur and nitrogen are released into the atmosphere. The main sources of these pollutants are power stations and car exhausts.

Sources of pollutants, 2011

▶ Transport
▶ Energy combustion
▶ Manufacturing industries

Nitrogen oxides
1%
37%
62%

Sulphur oxides
11%
14%
75%

National Institute of Statistics
www.istat.it
EUROSTAT
ec.europa.eu/eurostat
The Italian Park Portal
www.parks.it

World Heritage Site

Cinque Terre Marine Protected Area was created to protect natural features. Unique rock formations and rare species of coral are found on the seabed. It is also a sanctuary for whales.

Areas at risk from industrial pollution

Coastal areas most at risk from oil pollution

Main tourist area

National Park

Protected Area

● City with poor air quality

Scale 1 : 5 000 000

This is a simulated natural colour image of Venice and the surrounding area of northeast Italy. The image is made of hundreds of tiny frames which were taken at different times of the year. The brown, yellow and green colours of the land area shows how vegetation grew there between the time the first frame was taken and the time the last one was taken. In the same way the colours in the sea to the east of the image show changes in the height and pattern of the waves.

1 Venice and its lagoon. The city of Venice is the pale grey area.

2 Many cities in Europe have pollution problems like Venice.

3 Some of the sand, mud and silt is polluted by chemicals from industry and sewage.

4 Sand, mud and silt brought down by rivers like the Adige are deposited in the sea.

ASTER satellite images
asterweb.jpl.nasa.gov
Earth From Space
earth.jsc.nasa.gov/Collections/EarthFromSpace

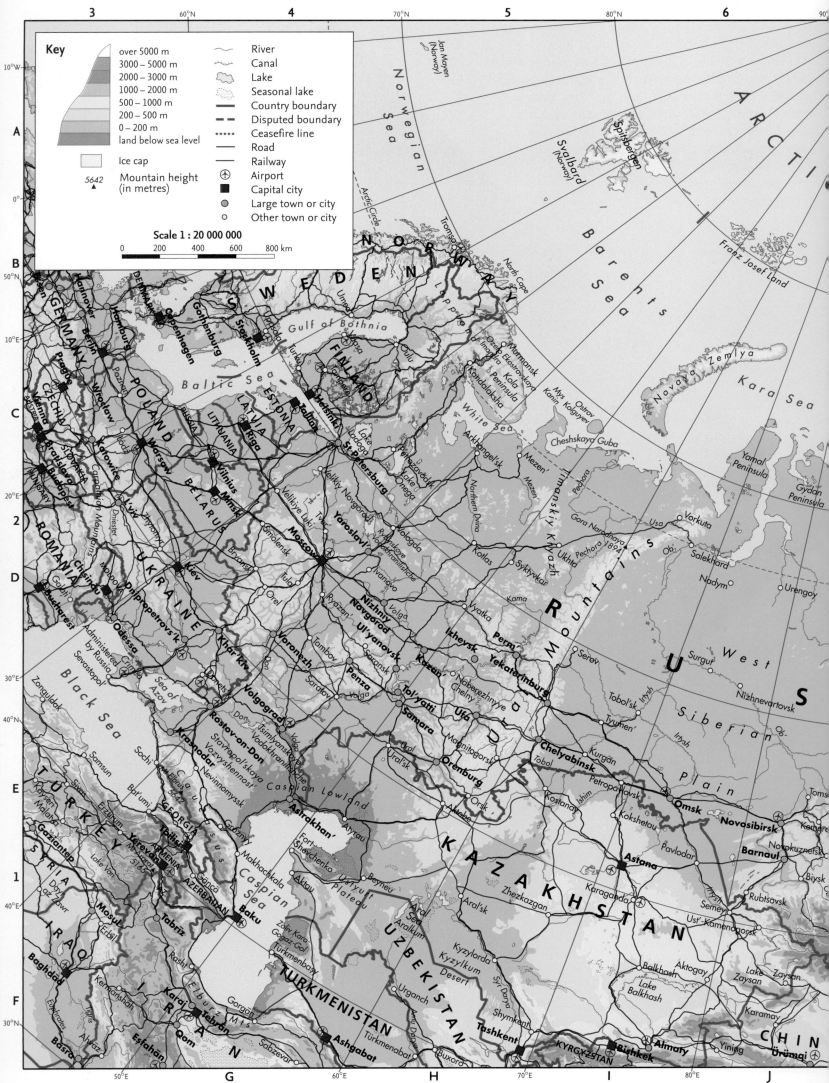

Key

over 5000 m	
3000 – 5000 m	
2000 – 3000 m	
1000 – 2000 m	
500 – 1000 m	
200 – 500 m	
0 – 200 m	
land below sea level	

Ice cap

5642 ▲ Mountain height (in metres)

〜 River
〜 Canal
Lake
Seasonal lake
—— Country boundary
– – – Disputed boundary
······ Ceasefire line
—— Road
—— Railway
⊕ Airport
■ Capital city
● Large town or city
○ Other town or city

Scale 1 : 20 000 000

0 200 400 600 800 km

Conic Equidistant Projection

Land use

- Urban
- Cropland
- Cropland and woodland
- Grassland and grazing
- Grassland and woodland
- Temperate forest
- Coniferous forest
- Scrubland or desert
- Swamp and marsh
- Tundra

Scale 1 : 50 000 000

Arctic Circle

Land use

43%   50%

7%

- Forest
- Arable
- Other

Agricultural production 2012

Million tonnes

Sugarbeet, Wheat, Milk, Potatoes, Barley, Maize, Sunflower seeds, Oats, Other vegetables

Main agricultural exports 2012

Million tonnes

Wheat, Barley, Sunflower cake, Maize, Wheat flour

Agricultural trading partners 2012

Egypt 1356
Turkey 924
Ukraine 662
Azerbaijan 542
Saudi Arabia 384
Israel 341
Italy 325
Uzbekistan 227
Kenya 175
Armenia 174

0   200   400   600   800   1000   1200   1400
Million US$

Energy

- Oilfield
- Gasfield
- Oil and gasfield
- Oil pipeline
- Gas pipeline

Scale 1 : 50 000 000

Arctic Circle

Fuel production 2014

Million tonnes of oil equivalent

600
500
400
300
200
100
0
Coal   Oil   Gas

World coal reserves 2014

27%
23%
4%
7%
8%
13%
18%

World oil reserves 2014

17%
21%
16%
6%
6%
9%
9%
10%

World gas reserves 2014

18%
33%
18%
4%
5%
9%
13%

- Australia
- Canada
- China
- Germany
- India
- Iran
- Iraq
- Kuwait
- Qatar
- Russia
- Saudi Arabia
- Turkmenistan
- UAE
- USA
- Venezuela
- Rest of the world

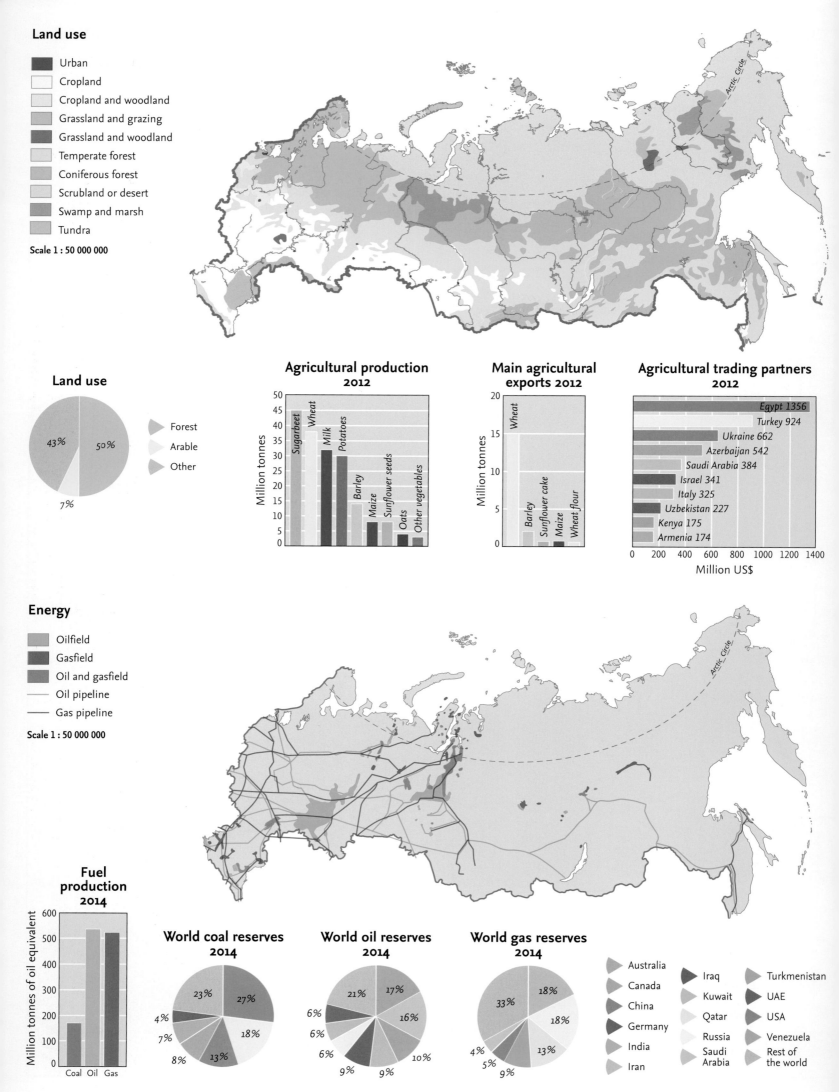

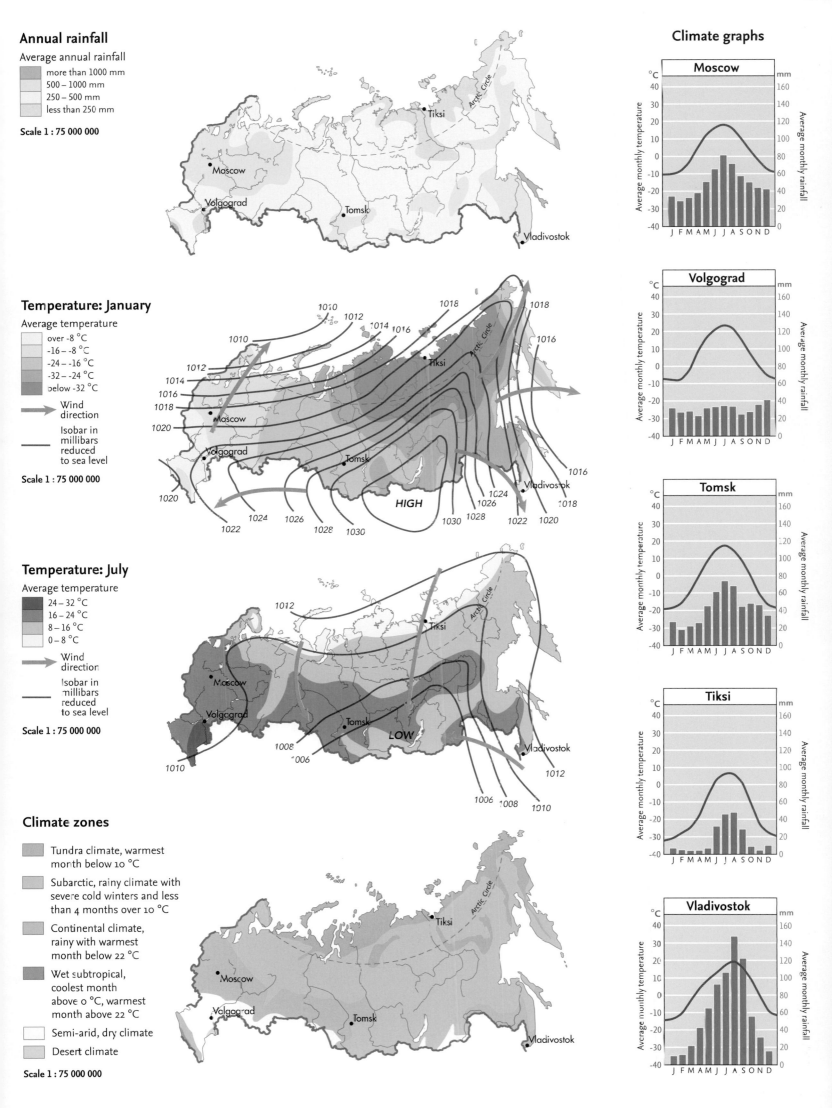

Annual rainfall

Average annual rainfall

- more than 1000 mm
- 500 – 1000 mm
- 250 – 500 mm
- less than 250 mm

Scale 1 : 75 000 000

Temperature: January

Average temperature

- over -8 °C
- -16 – -8 °C
- -24 – -16 °C
- -32 – -24 °C
- below -32 °C

→ Wind direction

— Isobar in millibars reduced to sea level

Scale 1 : 75 000 000

Temperature: July

Average temperature

- 24 – 32 °C
- 16 – 24 °C
- 8 – 16 °C
- 0 – 8 °C

→ Wind direction

— Isobar in millibars reduced to sea level

Scale 1 : 75 000 000

Climate zones

- Tundra climate, warmest month below 10 °C
- Subarctic, rainy climate with severe cold winters and less than 4 months over 10 °C
- Continental climate, rainy with warmest month below 22 °C
- Wet subtropical, coolest month above 0 °C, warmest month above 22 °C
- Semi-arid, dry climate
- Desert climate

Scale 1 : 75 000 000

Climate graphs

Moscow

Volgograd

Tomsk

Tiksi

Vladivostok

ARCTIC OCEAN

B
C
D
E
F
G H I J K L M N

Spitsbergen
Franz Josef Land
Severnaya Zemlya
New Siberia Islands
Wrangel Island
Laptev Sea

Arctic Circle
North Cape
Kola Peninsula
Barents Sea
Novaya Zemlya
Taymyr Peninsula
Verkhoyanskiy Khrebet
Khrebet Kolyma

EUROPE
Alps
Baltic Sea
Lake Ladoga
Lake Onega
North European Plain
Vistula
Carpathian Mts
Danube

Central Russian Uplands
Ural Mountains
Gora Narodnaya 1894
West Siberian Plain
Ob
Central Siberian Plateau
Nizhnyaya Tunguska
S i b e r i a
Khrebet Dzhugdzhur
Sea of Okhotsk

Volga
Don
Yenisey
Lena
Stanovoy Khrebet
Amur

Black Sea
Taurus Mts
Mount Ararat 5165
Caucasus
Lake Van
Lake Urmia
Caspian Sea
Elburz Mts
Aral Sea
Syr Darya
Lake Balkhash
Lake Zaysan
Ob'
Yenisey
Lake Baikal
Altai Mountains
Da Hinggan Ling
Manchuria

Dead Sea
Tigris
Euphrates
Dasht-e Kavir
Amu Darya
Tien Shan
Gobi Desert
Huang He
North China Plain
Bo Hai
Yellow Sea

An Nafūd
Hijaz
Zagros Mountains
The Gulf
Makran
Hindu Kush
Karakoram Ra.
K2 8611
Tarim Basin
Kunlun Shan
Plateau of Tibet
Chang Jiang
East China Sea
Okinawa

Arabian Peninsula
Asir
Rub' al Khālī
Gulf of Oman
Helmand
Sulaiman Range
Indus
Sutlej
Himalaya
Annapurna 8091
Mount Everest 8848
Gonnga Shan 7514
Nan Ling
Taiwan

Jazirat Maşirah
Thar Desert
Narmada
Ganges
Brahmaputra
Irrawaddy
Xi Jiang
Luzon Strait

Arabian Sea
Socotra
Deccan
Western Ghats
Eastern Ghats
Bay of Bengal
Mouths of the Ganges
Mouths of the Irrawaddy
Hainan
South China Sea
Luzon
Philippines

Laccadive Islands
Sri Lanka
Andaman Islands
Andaman Sea
Gulf of Thailand
Palawan
Sulu Sea

Maldives
Nicobar Islands
Strait of Malacca
Peninsular Malaysia
Celebes Sea

Chagos Archipelago
INDIAN OCEAN
Kepulauan Mentawai
Sumatra
Borneo
Java Sea
Celebes

Java
Bali
Lombok
Flores

Key

over 5000 m
3000 – 5000 m
2000 – 3000 m
1000 – 2000 m
500 – 1000 m
200 – 500 m
0 – 200 m
land below sea level

Ice cap

▲ 8848 Mountain height (in metres)

Scale 1 : 40 000 000

0   500   1000   1500 km

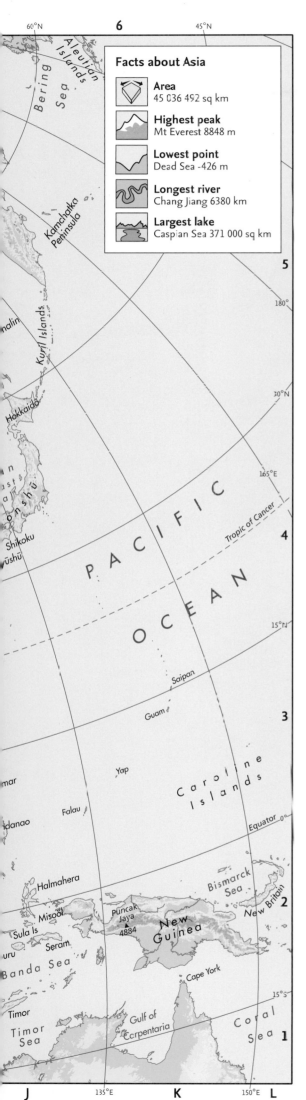

Facts about Asia

Area
45 036 492 sq km

Highest peak
Mt Everest 8848 m

Lowest point
Dead Sea -426 m

Longest river
Chang Jiang 6380 km

Largest lake
Caspian Sea 371 000 sq km

Countries

AR.   ARMENIA
AZ.   AZERBAIJAN
B.   BAHRAIN
BAN.   BANGLADESH
C.   CYPRUS
IS.   ISRAEL
L.   LEBANON
Q.   QATAR
U.A.E.   UNITED ARAB EMIRATES

Scale 1 : 80 000 000

India satellite image

The red box on the map opposite shows the area of the image below.

1 Sri Lanka is the large island off the southeastern coast of India. The bright colours show that it is mountainous especially in the southwestern part of the island.

2 The river Ganges enters the sea in the Bay of Bengal. The river can be seen as a thin blue line. Where the river enters the sea a large delta has formed.

3 The snow covered Himalaya stand out clearly in northern India.

4 The valley of the river Indus in Pakistan stands out on this image as a dark brown area.

@ **MODIS web imagery**
modis.gsfc.nasa.gov
Visible Earth
visibleearth.nasa.gov

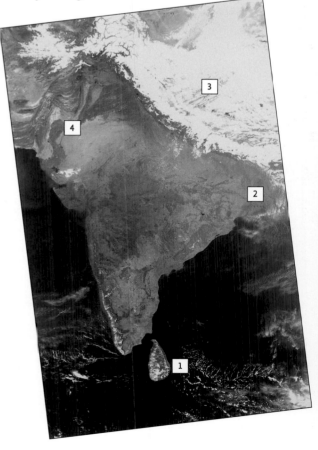

Lambert Azimuthal Equal Area projection

Key

| over 5000 m |
| 3000 – 5000 m |
| 2000 – 3000 m |
| 1000 – 2000 m |
| 500 – 1000 m |
| 200 – 500 m |
| 0 – 200 m |
| land below sea level |

Ice cap

8848 ▲ Mountain height (in metres)

～ River

～ Seasonal river

Lake

Seasonal lake

― Country boundary

- - - Disputed boundary

⋯⋯ Ceasefire line

― Road

― Railway

✈ Airport

■ Capital city

● Large town or city

○ Other town or city

Scale 1 : 20 000 000

0   200   400   600   800 km

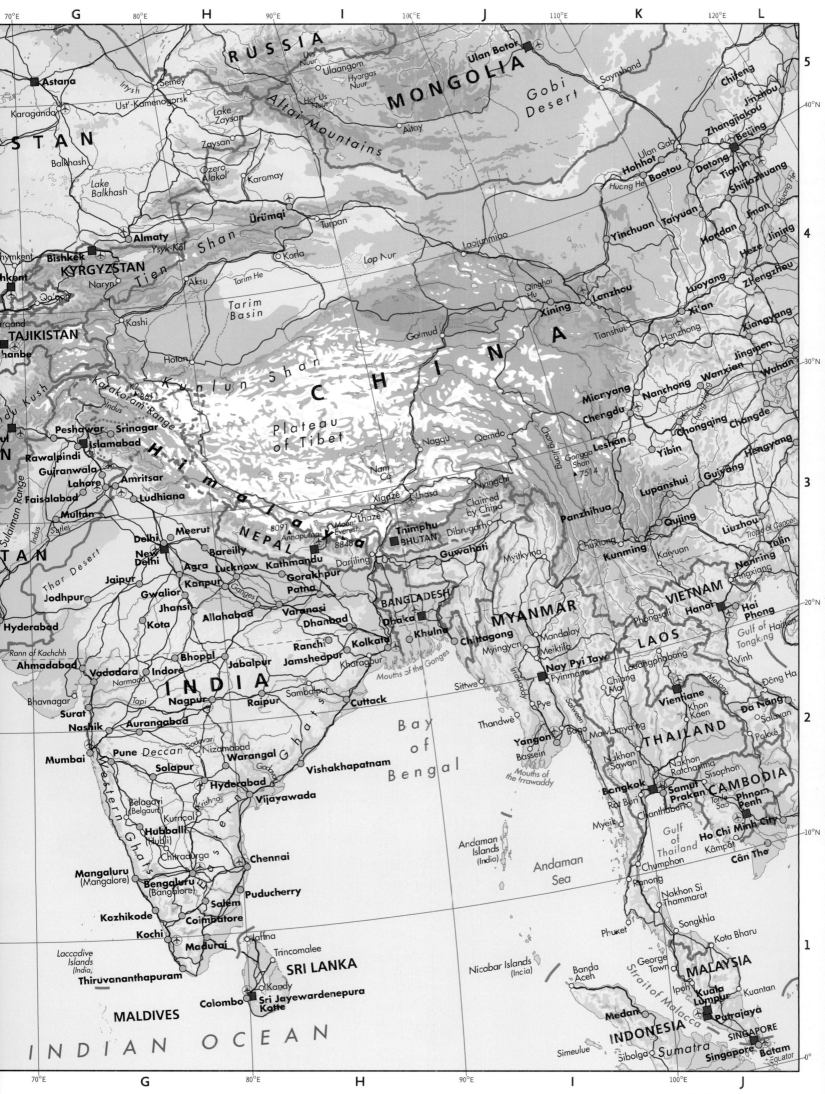

Food and agriculture

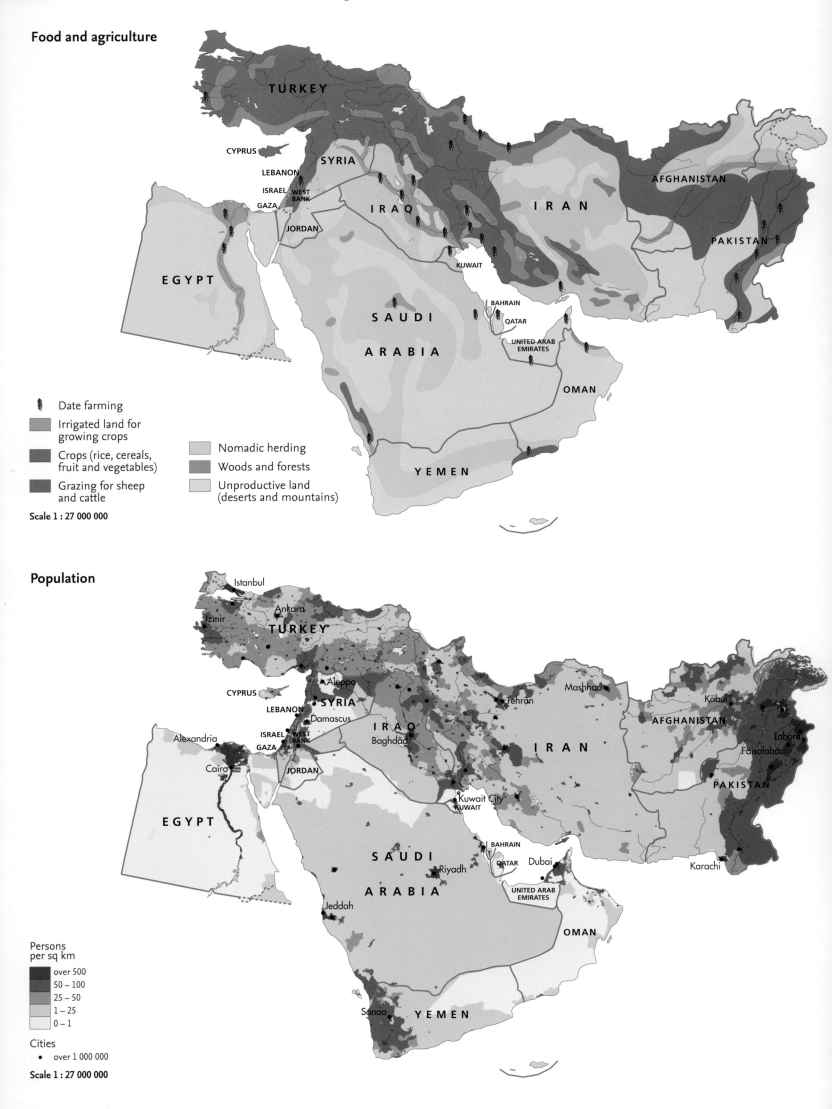

TURKEY

CYPRUS

SYRIA

LEBANON

ISRAEL
WEST
BANK
GAZA

JORDAN

EGYPT

IRAQ

IRAN

AFGHANISTAN

PAKISTAN

KUWAIT

BAHRAIN

QATAR

SAUDI

ARABIA

UNITED ARAB
EMIRATES

OMAN

YEMEN

Date farming

Irrigated land for
growing crops

Crops (rice, cereals,
fruit and vegetables)

Grazing for sheep
and cattle

Nomadic herding

Woods and forests

Unproductive land
(deserts and mountains)

Scale 1 : 27 000 000

Population

Istanbul

Ankara

Izmir

TURKEY

CYPRUS

Aleppo

LEBANON

SYRIA

Damascus

ISRAEL
WEST
BANK
GAZA

Alexandria

Cairo

JORDAN

EGYPT

IRAQ

Baghdad

Tehran

Mashhad

IRAN

Kābul

AFGHANISTAN

Lahore

Faisalabad

PAKISTAN

Karachi

Kuwait City
KUWAIT

BAHRAIN

QATAR

Dubai

SAUDI

Riyadh

ARABIA

UNITED ARAB
EMIRATES

Jeddah

OMAN

Sanaa

YEMEN

**Persons
per sq km**

over 500

50 – 100

25 – 50

1 – 25

0 – 1

Cities

• over 1 000 000

Scale 1 : 27 000 000

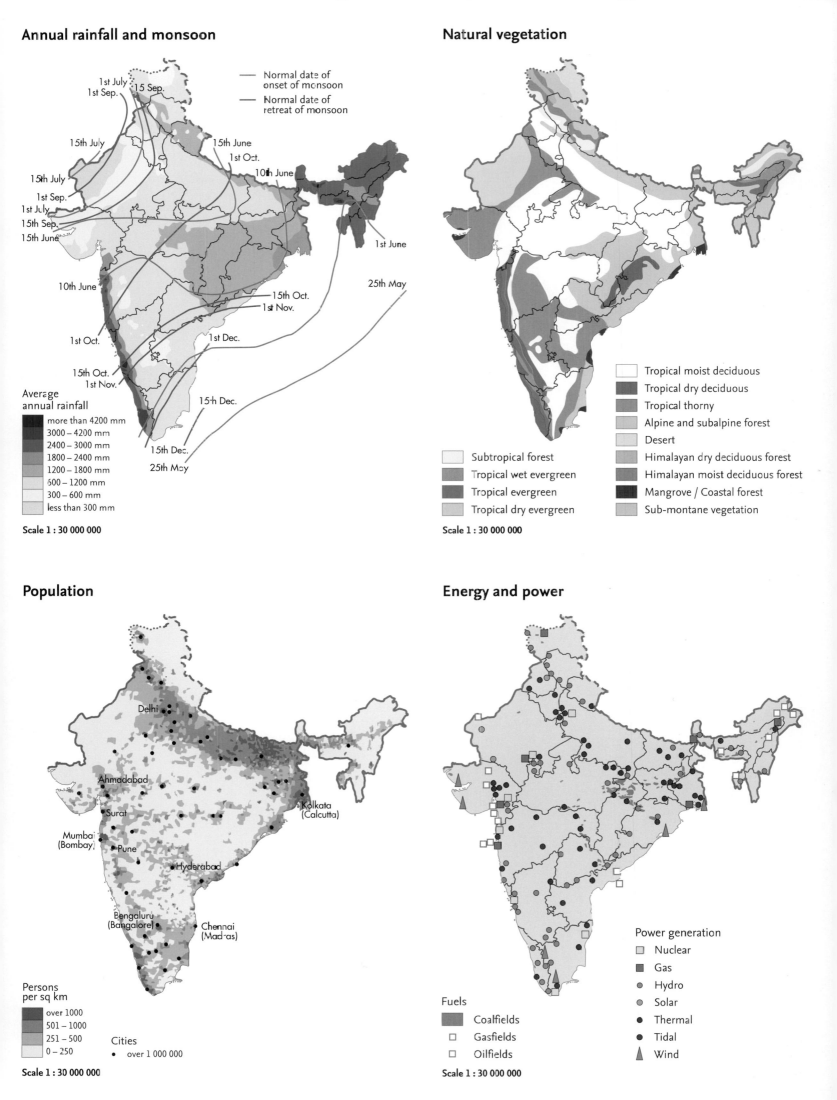

Annual rainfall and monsoon

—— Normal date of onset of monsoon
—— Normal date of retreat of monsoon

1st July
1st Sep.
15 Sep.
15th July
15th June
1st Oct.
10th June
15th July
1st Sep.
1st July
15th Sep.
15th June
1st June
10th June
25th May
15th Oct.
1st Nov.
1st Oct.
1st Dec.
15th Oct.
1st Nov.
15th Dec.
15th Dec.
25th May

Average annual rainfall

- more than 4200 mm
- 3000 – 4200 mm
- 2400 – 3000 mm
- 1800 – 2400 mm
- 1200 – 1800 mm
- 600 – 1200 mm
- 300 – 600 mm
- less than 300 mm

Scale 1 : 30 000 000

Natural vegetation

- Subtropical forest
- Tropical wet evergreen
- Tropical evergreen
- Tropical dry evergreen
- Tropical moist deciduous
- Tropical dry deciduous
- Tropical thorny
- Alpine and subalpine forest
- Desert
- Himalayan dry deciduous forest
- Himalayan moist deciduous forest
- Mangrove / Coastal forest
- Sub-montane vegetation

Scale 1 : 30 000 000

Population

Delhi
Ahmadabad
Surat
Mumbai (Bombay)
Pune
Hyderabad
Kolkata (Calcutta)
Bengaluru (Bangalore)
Chennai (Madras)

Persons per sq km

- over 1000
- 501 – 1000
- 251 – 500
- 0 – 250

Cities
- • over 1 000 000

Scale 1 : 30 000 000

Energy and power

Power generation

- □ Nuclear
- ■ Gas
- ● Hydro
- ● Solar
- ● Thermal
- ● Tidal
- ▲ Wind

Fuels

- Coalfields
- □ Gasfields
- □ Oilfields

Scale 1 : 30 000 000

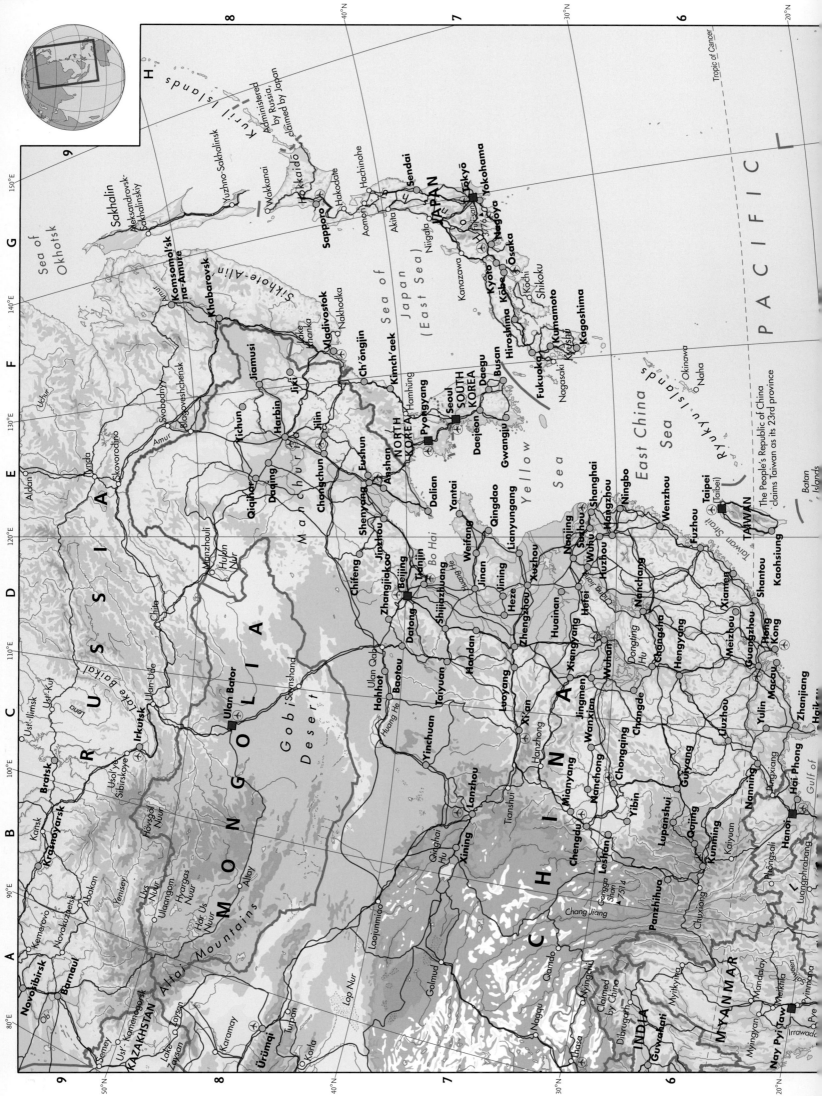

PACIFIC

Kuril Islands
Administered by Russia, claimed by Japan

Sea of Okhotsk

Sakhalin
Aleksandrovsk-Sakhalinskiy
Yuzhno-Sakhalinsk

Wakkanai
Hokkaidō
Hakodate
Sapporo
Hachinohe
Aomori
Akita
Sendai
Niigata
Kanazawa
Tōkyō
Yokohama
Nagoya
HONSHU
JAPAN
Kyōto
Kōbe
Ōsaka
Kōchi
Shikoku
Hiroshima
Kumamoto
Fukuoka
Nagasaki
Kyūshū
Kagoshima

Sea of Japan (East Sea)

Komsomol'sk na-Amure
Khabarovsk
Sikhote-Alin
Vladivostok
Nakhodka
Ch'ŏngjin
Kimch'aek
Hamhŭng
Pyongyang
NORTH KOREA
Seoul
SOUTH KOREA
Daejeon
Daegu
Busan
Gwangju

Jiamusi
Jixi
Yichun
Harbin
Jilin
Qiqihar
Daqing
Changchun
Fushun
Manchuria
Shenyang
Anshan
Jinzhou
Dalian
Yantai
Qingdao
Weifang
Jinan
Lianyungang

Yellow Sea

East China Sea

Ryukyu Islands
Okinawa
Naha

Tropic of Cancer

Batan Islands

Taipei (Taibei)
TAIWAN
Kaohsiung

The People's Republic of China claims Taiwan as its 23rd province.

Aldan
Lena
Tynda
Skovorodino
Svobodnyy
Blagoveshchensk
Amur
Manzhouli
Hulun Nur

RUSSIA

Ust'-Kut
Ust'-Ilimsk
Bratsk
Lake Baikal
Irkutsk
Ulan-Ude
Usol'ye Sibirskoye

Bratsk
Kansk
Krasnoyarsk
Yenisey
Abakan
Kemerovo
Novokuznetsk
Novosibirsk
Barnaul

Biysk
Rubtsovsk
Semey
Lake Zaysan

KAZAKHSTAN

Ölgiy
Hyargas Nuur
Uvs Nuur
Üüreg Nuur
Höwsgöl Nuur
Ulaangom
Hö Us Nuur
Altay
Altai Mountains

MONGOLIA

Ulan Bator
Sühbaatar
Gobi Desert

Chifeng
Zhangjiakou
Ulan Qab
Hohhot
Baotou
Huang He
Datong
Beijing
Tianjin
Bo Hai
Shijiazhuang
Handan
Taiyuan
Yinchuan
Qinghai Hu
Xining
Lanzhou
Tianshui
Hanzhong
Xi'an
Luoyang
Zhengzhou
Heze
Jining
Xuzhou

CHINA

Hezhou
Huaian
Nanjing
Suzhou
Wuxi
Hefei
Huai He
Xiangyang
Jingmen
Wanxian
Nanchong
Chengdu
Mianyang
Chongqing
Changde
Dongting Hu
Wuhan
Nanchang
Hangzhou
Shanghai
Ningbo
Wenzhou
Fuzhou
Hengyang
Changsha
Guiyang
Liuzhou
Guilin
Shaoguan
Guangzhou
Hong Kong
Macau
Shantou
Xiamen

Taiwan Strait

Kunming
Qujing
Lupanshui
Panzhihua
Leshan
Yibin
Gongga Shan 7514
Chang Jiang
Qamdo
Nyingchi

Qinghai Hu
Golmud
Lap Nur
Laojunmiao
Karamay
Ürümqi
Turpan
Turpan
Korla

50°N
40°N
30°N
20°N

Nagqu
Lhasa
Claimed by China
Dibrugarh
Guwahati
INDIA

MYANMAR
Mandalay
Myingyan
Nay Pyi Taw
Meiktila
Myitkyina
Pyinmana
Pye
Phôngsali
Luangphrabang
Hanoi
Hai Phong
Gulf of Tonkin
Zhanjiang
Haikou

Yulin
Nanning
Beihai

80°E 90°E 100°E 110°E 120°E 130°E 140°E 150°E

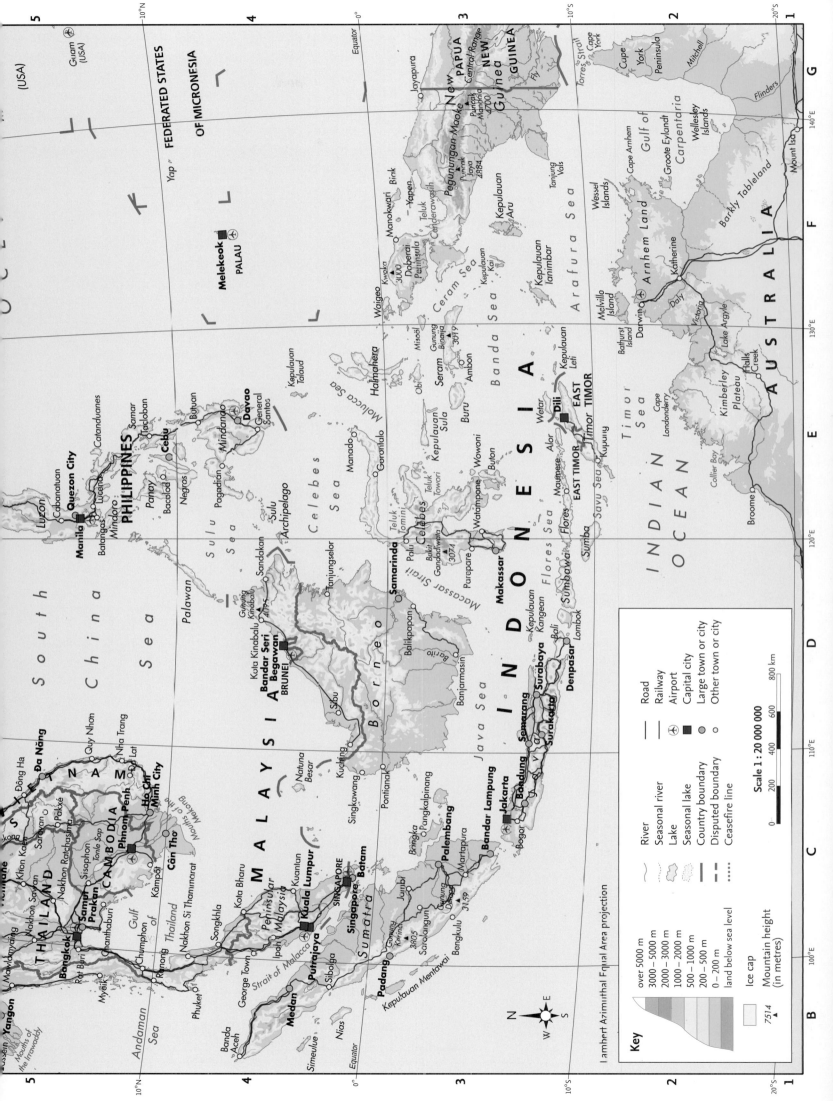

Key

Road

Railway

✈ **Airport**

■ **Capital city**

● **Large town or city**

○ **Other town or city**

River

Seasonal river

Lake

Seasonal lake

Country boundary

Disputed boundary

Ceasefire line

Scale 1 : 20 000 000

0   200   400   600   800 km

over 5000 m
3000 – 5000 m
2000 – 3000 m
1000 – 2000 m
500 – 1000 m
200 – 500 m
0 – 200 m
land below sea level

Ice cap

7514 ▲ Mountain height
(in metres)

Lambert Azimuthal Equal Area projection

N
W E
S

Facts about Japan

Landscape
Area: 377 727 sq km
Highest point: Fuji-san 3776 m

Population
Total: 126 573 000
Density: 335 persons per sq km

Settlement
% Urban population: 94
Main towns: Tōkyō, Ōsaka-Kōbe,
Nagoya, Fukuoka-Kita-Kyūshū

Land use
Main crops: Rice, potatoes, sugar beets
Main industries: Electrical equipment,
transport equipment, other machinery,
chemicals

Development indicators
Life expectancy: male 80, female 87
GNI per capita: US$ 42 000
Primary school enrolment ratio: 100
% Access to safe water: 100

Key

3000 – 5000 m	
2000 – 3000 m	
1000 – 2000 m	
500 – 1000 m	
200 – 500 m	
0 – 200 m	

——— Country boundary
- - - Disputed boundary
········ Ceasefire line
——— Road
——— Railway
⊕ Airport
■ Capital city
◉ Large town or city
○ Other town or city
▲ 3776 Mountain height (in metres)
River
Lake

Japanese name forms

-dake	peak
-hanto	peninsula
-jima	island
-kai	bay, inlet
-kaikyo	strait
-ko	lake
-nada	sea, gulf
-retto	chain of islands
-san	mountain
-sanchi	mountainous area
-shima	island
-suido	strait, channel
-to	island
-wan	sea
-yama	mountain

Scale 1 : 7 500 000

0   100   200   300   400 km

Albers Equal Area Conic projection

Annual rainfall

The driest parts of Japan are in the north, on the island of Hokkaidō. Most rain falls on the high mountain tops and the southern and western coasts.

Average annual rainfall

- more than 3000 mm
- 2000 – 3000 mm
- 1500 – 2000 mm
- 1000 – 1500 mm
- less than 1000 mm

Scale 1 : 15 000 000

Land use

Over 66% of this steep-sided mountainous country is covered by forest. Flat land, suitable for agriculture, is in very short supply and as a result farming is intensive in order to maximise production.

- Rice
- Tea
- Mulberry
- Orchards
- Upland fields
- Forest
- Built-up

Scale 1 : 15 000 000

Land use by category

- Forest
- Farmland
- Built-up
- Water
- Grassland
- Other

8%
1%
4%
9%
12%
66%

Population

Japan has a high overall population density. There are huge contrasts in density between the land suitable for urban development and the unspoilt forested and wilderness areas in the northern islands.

Persons per sq km

- over 250
- 100 – 250
- 10 – 100
- 0 – 10

Cities

- ● over 25 000 000
- ● 10 000 000 – 25 000 000
- • 1 000 000 – 10 000 000

Scale 1 : 15 000 000

Economic activity

Tōkyō and its surrounding area is the main economic heart of Japan. Electronics and car manufacturing are major industries. The primary sector of the economy is very small due to a lack of natural resources.

Industry
- Iron / Steel
- Oil refineries
- Shipbuilding
- Motor vehicles
- Mechanical engineering
- Electronics
- Publishing / Paper
- Chemicals
- Textiles / Clothing
- Food processing
- • Major industrial centre

Service industry
- S Banking and finance

Scale 1 : 15 000 000

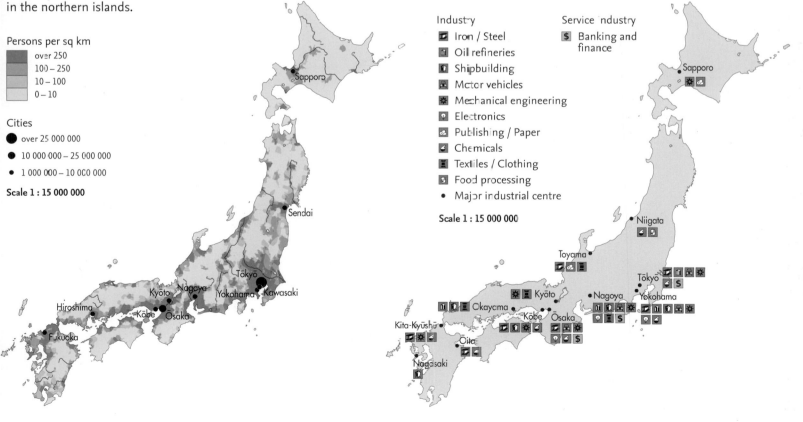

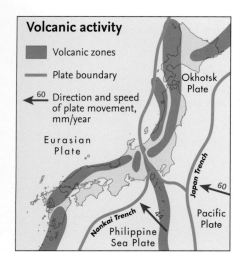

Volcanic activity

Volcanic zones

Plate boundary

→ 60 Direction and speed of plate movement, mm/year

Okhotsk Plate

Eurasian Plate

Japan Trench

Nankai Trench

60

44

Philippine Sea Plate

Pacific Plate

Japan is situated on the 'Ring of Fire' around the Pacific Ocean. There are almost 200 volcanoes in the 'Ring of Fire' and over 20 are still active. Earthquakes are more disastrous than volcanic eruptions in Japan where 5000 earthquakes are recorded annually. The main earthquake zones lie on the Pacific side of Japan. Strong earthquakes may destroy roads and railways, collapse houses and result in many casualties.

Earthquake seismogram

A seismogram is used to record the horizontal or vertical vibration caused during the course of an earthquake. The vertical divisions represent time intervals of 5 seconds.

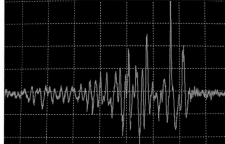

Richter scale

The scale of measurement used to describe the strength of an earthquake is known as the Richter Scale. The scale measures the energy which is released at the centre of an earthquake. Every year about 50 000 quakes measuring 3 – 4 are recorded worldwide, while only 800 measuring 5 – 6 occur.

9	Over 8.0 most powerful earthquake
8	
7	7.0 – 8.0 major earthquake
6	6.0 – 7.0 destructive earthquake
5	4.5 – 6.0 earthquake causes local damage
4	3.5 – 4.5 earthquake felt by many people
3	2.5 – 3.5 earthquake recorded but not felt
2	below 2.5 earthquake not recorded
1	
0	

Volcanic rocks

▲ Active volcano (erupted since 1850)

△ Other volcano

● Earthquakes greater than magnitude 6 since 1900

Scale 1 : 9 000 000

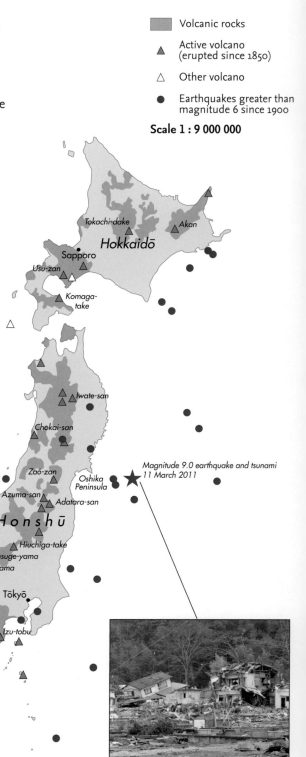

Magnitude 9.0 earthquake and tsunami 11 March 2011

Tōhoku earthquake

The most powerful earthquake ever to hit Japan, with a magnitude of 9 on the Richter Scale, occurred in March 2011. Its epicentre was 70 km east of the Oshika Peninsula. The earthquake created huge tsunami waves that caused widespread destruction on Japan's Pacific coast. Nearly 20 000 people were killed as a result of the earthquake and tsunami. The tsunami also caused a number of nuclear accidents, the worst of which was in Fukushima.

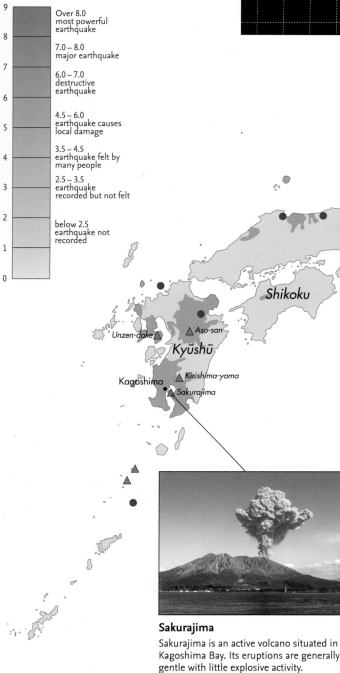

Sakurajima

Sakurajima is an active volcano situated in Kagoshima Bay. Its eruptions are generally gentle with little explosive activity.

Fuji

Situated on the island of Honshū, Fuji is a dormant volcano which has not erupted since 1707. At 3776 m, it is the highest mountain in Japan and has a crater which is 610 metres in diameter.

USGS National Earthquake Information Center earthquake.usgs.gov
Earthquake Research Institute www.eri.u-tokyo.ac.jp/eng

This image of Sakurajima volcano was taken by a Landsat satellite. The image uses false colours to highlight the contrasts in the different ways in which the land is used. Black is used to show those parts of the image which are sea. Towns and urban areas are shown in pink, and mountains and forests show up in dark grey-greens.

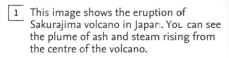

1   This image shows the eruption of Sakurajima volcano in Japan. You can see the plume of ash and steam rising from the centre of the volcano.

2   The city of Kirishima lies to the north of the volcano and is shown in pink, purple and brown on the satellite image.

3   The Sakurajima volcano has built up an island 10 km wide in Kagoshima Bay. As the island has grown bigger it has joined on to the land to the east of the bay.

4   The city of Kagoshima lies to the west of the volcano. Ash from the volcano often falls on the houses, shops, offices and factories of the city.

 Sakurajima Volcano Research Center
www.svc.dpri.kyoto-u.ac.jp/default_e.html

Landscape

The landscape of China ranges from high mountains and plateaux in the west to lower plains in the east. Its major rivers flow from west to east towards the Pacific Ocean.

Facts about China

Landscape
Area: 9 584 492 sq km
Highest point: Gongga Shan 7514 m

Population
Total: 1 383 925 000
Density: 144 persons per sq km

Settlement
% Urban population: 57
Main towns/cities: Beijing, Shanghai, Wuhan, Guangzhou, Shenzhen

Land use
Main crops: Rice, wheat, potatoes, corn, peanuts
Main industries: Electrical and other machinery, clothing, textiles, iron and steel

Development indicators
Life expectancy: male 74, female 77
GNI per capita: US$ 7380
Primary school enrolment ratio: 99
% Access to safe water: 92

Earthquake zones

China is located in one of the most active seismic regions of the world. In the Tangshan earthquake, in 1976, over 240 000 people lost their lives and more recently, in 2008, 80 000 people were killed during the earthquake in Sichuan Province.

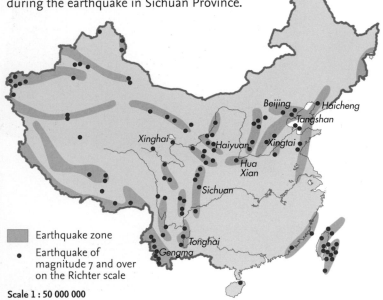

Earthquake zone

● Earthquake of magnitude 7 and over on the Richter scale

Scale 1 : 50 000 000

Population

China has been the world's most populous nation for many centuries. In the early 1970s, the government implemented a stringent one-child birth-control policy in an attempt to slow down the population growth rate which is now more stable. Life expectancy has risen and China has an increasingly ageing population.

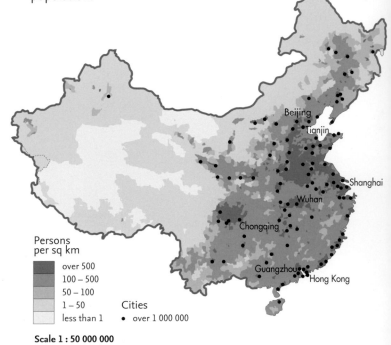

Persons per sq km

over 500
100 – 500
50 – 100
1 – 50
less than 1

Cities
● over 1 000 000

Scale 1 : 50 000 000

Population change

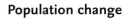

- Total population
- Birth rate
- Natural increase rate
- Death rate

Population structure

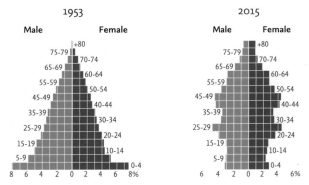

1953
Male | Female

2015
Male | Female

Each full square represents 1% of the total population

Environmental pollution

Rapid industrial development and an increase in energy consumption in China has resulted in serious pollution problems such as smog and degradation of natural resources.

Many of the world's most polluted cities are in China. Acid rain falls on nearly one third of the country.

Soil degradation and desertification

Almost all of China's rivers are polluted to some degree. Overgrazing and the expansion of agricultural land has led to serious desertification in northern China.

Plans to combat these problems include forest planting schemes, pollution control projects and the installation of rubbish treatment plants.

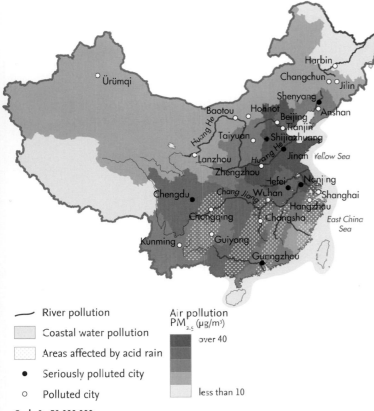

River pollution

Coastal water pollution

Areas affected by acid rain

● Seriously polluted city

○ Polluted city

Air pollution
PM$_{2.5}$ (µg/m³)
over 40
less than 10

Scale 1 : 50 000 000

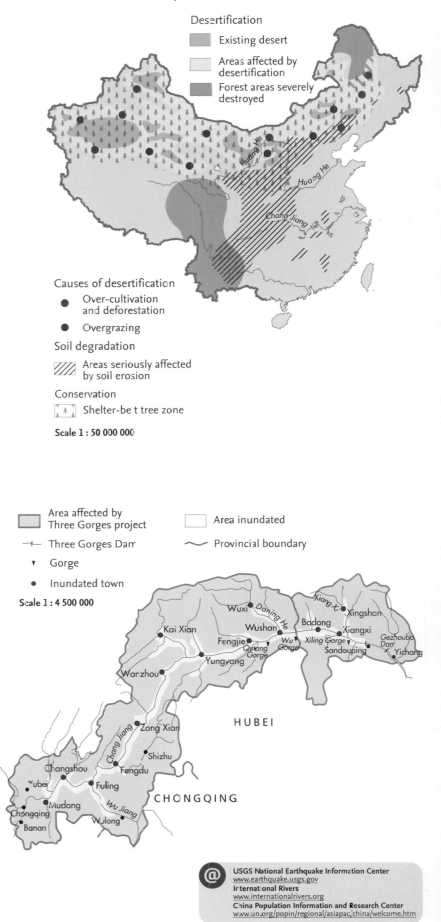

Desertification
- Existing desert
- Areas affected by desertification
- Forest areas severely destroyed

Causes of desertification
● Over-cultivation and deforestation
● Overgrazing

Soil degradation
Areas seriously affected by soil erosion

Conservation
Shelter-belt tree zone

Scale 1 : 50 000 000

Area affected by Three Gorges project

Area inundated

Three Gorges Dam

Provincial boundary

▼ Gorge

● Inundated town

Scale 1 : 4 500 000

Three Gorges Dam

The Three Gorges Dam, spanning the Chang Jiang in China, is the largest hydroelectric power project in the world. The dam body was completed in 2006 and the length of the reservoir is 600 kilometres. The project produces clean electricity, prevents deadly floods downstream and improves navigation.

The dam has also flooded archaeological and cultural sites and displaced some 1.24 million people and is causing dramatic ecological changes.

An aerial view of the Three Gorges Dam with the dam clearly visible in the bottom right hand corner.

USGS National Earthquake Information Center
www.earthquake.usgs.gov
International Rivers
www.internationalrivers.org
China Population Information and Research Center
www.un.org/popin/regional/asiapac/china/welcome.htm

Facts about Africa

Area
30 343 578 sq km

Highest peak
Kilimanjaro 5892 m

Lowest point
Lake Assal -156 m

Longest river
Nile 6695 km

Largest lake
Lake Victoria 68 800 sq km

EUROPE

Bay of Biscay
Cape Finisterre
Madeira
Douro
Tagus
Cabo de São Vicente
Canary Islands
C. Blanc
C. Vert
Sénégal
Gambia
Fouta Djallon
Cape Palmas
Madeira
Pyrenees
Ebro
Balearic Is
Majorca
Corsica
Sardinia
Alps
Apennines
Adriatic Sea
Sicily
Crete
Cyprus
Black Sea
Danube
Taurus Mts
Lake Tuz
Mediterranean Sea
G. of Gabès
Gulf of Sirte
Nile Delta
Suez Canal
Sinai
Dead Sea
Qattara Depression
Libyan Desert
An Nafūd
ASIA
Arabian Peninsula
Asīr
Rub' al Khālī
The Gulf
Tropic of Cancer
Nile
Lake Nasser
Nubian Desert
Red Sea
Hijaz
Jbel Toubkal 4167
Atlas Mountains
Sahara
Mont Tahat 2918
Ahaggar
Djado Plateau
Mt Gréboun 1800
Massif de l'Aïr
Tibesti
Emi Koussi 3415
Niger
Bani
Black Volta
White Volta
Niger
Lake Volta
Bight of Benin
Gulf of Guinea
Bioco
Príncipe
São Tomé
Jos Plateau
Benue
Adamawa Highlands
Mt Cameroun 4100
Lake Chad
Chari
Logone
Darfur
Jebel Marra 3088
Sudd
Blue Nile
Gezira
Lake Tana
Ras Dejen 4533
Lake Assal
Ethiopian Highlands
Gulf of Aden
Socotra
White Nile
Atbara
Akobo
Webi Shabeelle
Jubba
Lake Turkana
Uele
Ubangi
Sangha
Aruwimi
Congo
Congo Basin
Congo
Kasai
Kwilu
Cuango
Cuanza
Lake Albert
Lake Edward
Margherita Peak 5110
Lake Victoria
Mount Kenya 5199
Kilimanjaro 5892
Masai Steppe
Equator
INDIAN OCEAN
Pemba Island
Zanzibar Island
Mafia Island
Rufiji
Aldabra Islands
Lake Tanganyika
Lake Mweru
Great Rift Valley
Muchinga Mts
Lake Nyasa
Comoro Islands
ATLANTIC OCEAN
Ascension
St Helena
Bié Plateau
Cunene
Cubango
Namib Desert
Etosha Pan
Okavango Delta
Kalahari Desert
Zambezi
Victoria Falls
Lake Kariba
Matabele Upland
Zambezi
Save
Limpopo
Mozambique Channel
Madagascar
Maur
Réunion
Tropic of Capricorn
Orange
Vaal
Thabana-Ntlenyana 3482
Drakensberg
Great Karoo
Cape of Good Hope
Cape Agulhas

Key

over 5000 m
3000 – 5000 m
2000 – 3000 m
1000 – 2000 m
500 – 1000 m
200 – 500 m
0 – 200 m
land below sea level

5892 ▲ Mountain height (in metres)

Scale 1 : 37 000 000

0   500   1000   1500 km

N
W   E
S

Lambert Azimuthal Equal Area projection

This is an infra-red satellite image of the delta of the river Nile, the Sinai peninsula and the neighbouring parts of Israel, Jordan and Saudi Arabia. Most of this area is desert and this is shown in the pale pinky-brown colour. The red colour in the delta of the river Nile shows that most of the land here is used for farming. The pale blue areas on the edge of the delta are shallow lagoons.

1 The city of Cairo is the dark grey area at the base of the delta.

2 The valley of the river Nile is shown as a dark line which ends at the delta.

3 The Suez Canal was built in 1869 by connecting a series of lakes which are shown in black. The Suez Canal allows ships to sail from the Mediterranean Sea, in the north of the image, to the Red Sea.

4 The Red Sea is shown in black on the image. The pale grey areas in the sea are islands.

5 The Dead Sea in Israel is shown in black on the satellite image.

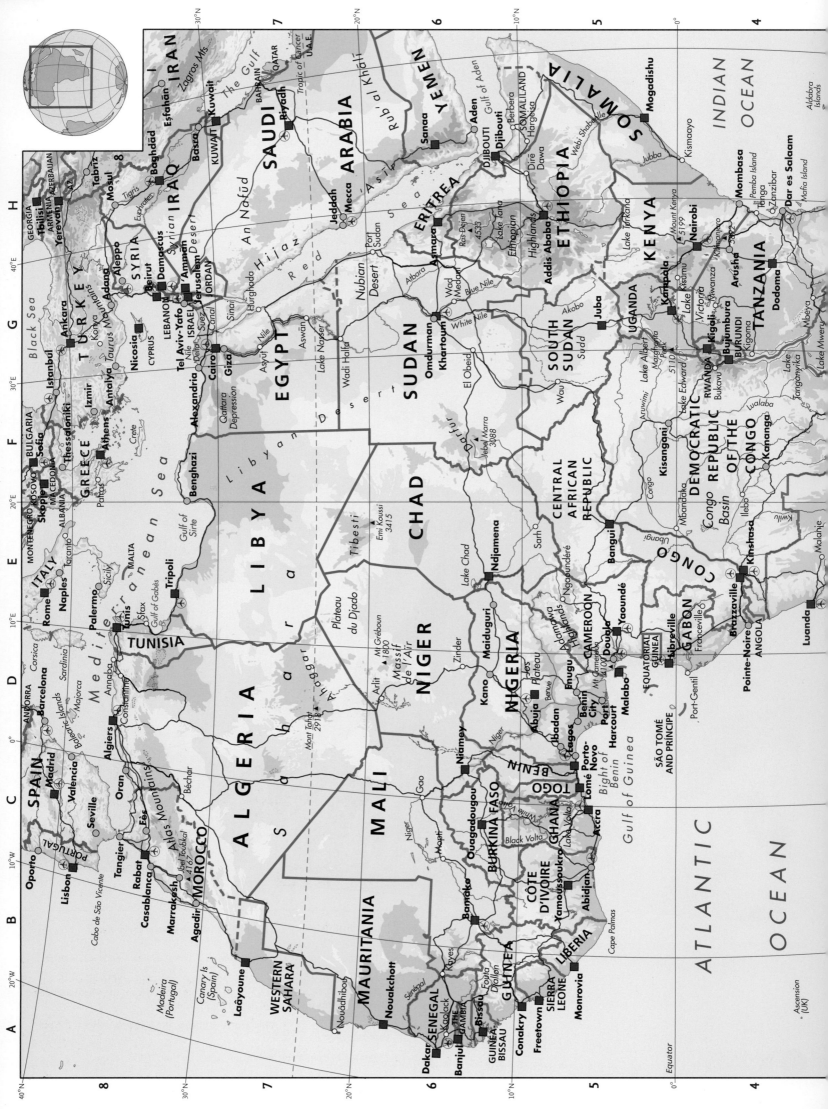

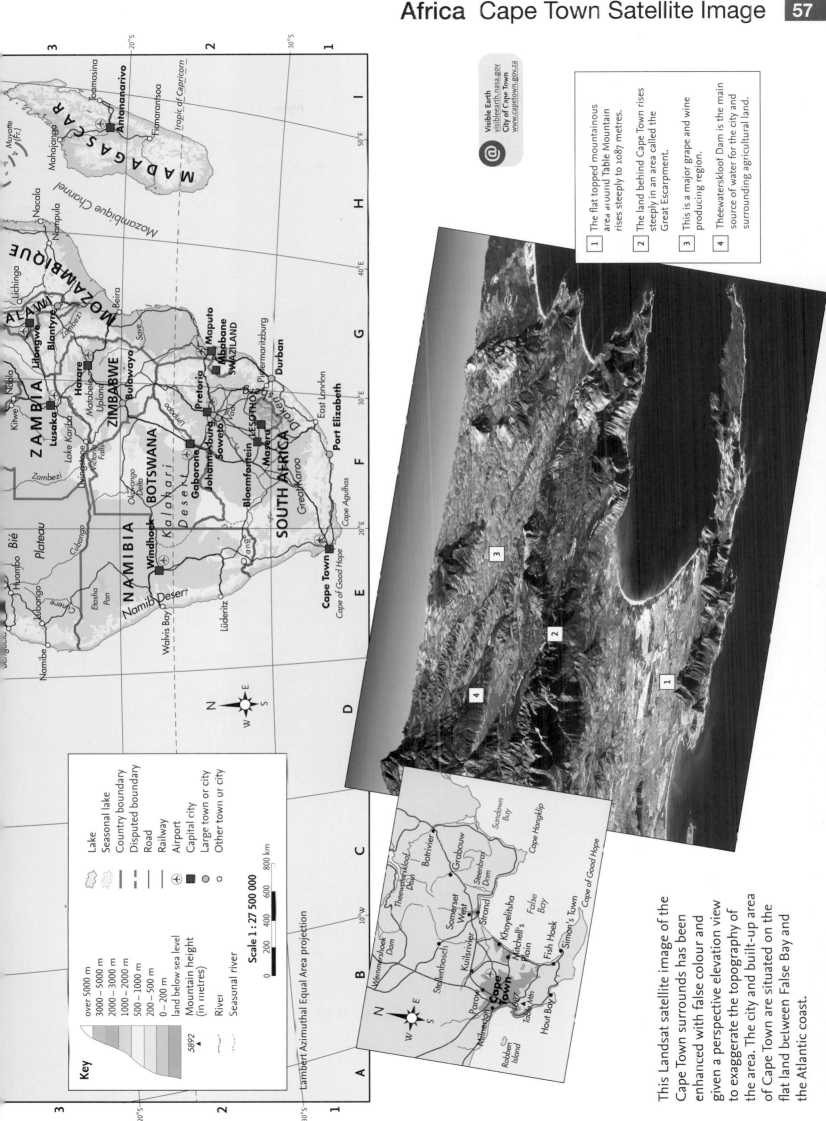

Visible Earth
visibleearth.nasa.gov
City of Cape Town
www.capetown.gov.za

1 The flat topped mountainous area around Table Mountain rises steeply to 1087 metres.

2 The land behind Cape Town rises steeply in an area called the Great Escarpment.

3 This is a major grape and wine producing region.

4 Theewaterskloof Dam is the main source of water for the city and surrounding agricultural land.

This Landsat satellite image of the Cape Town surrounds has been enhanced with false colour and given a perspective elevation view to exaggerate the topography of the area. The city and built-up area of Cape Town are situated on the flat land between False Bay and the Atlantic coast.

Key

	Lake
	Seasonal lake
	Country boundary
	Disputed boundary
	Road
	Railway
✈	Airport
■	Capital city
●	Large town or city
○	Other town or city

over 5000 m
3000 – 5000 m
2000 – 3000 m
1000 – 2000 m
500 – 1000 m
200 – 500 m
0 – 200 m
land below sea level

5892 ▲ Mountain height (in metres)

River
Seasonal river

Scale 1 : 27 500 000

0   200   400   600   800 km

Lambert Azimuthal Equal Area projection

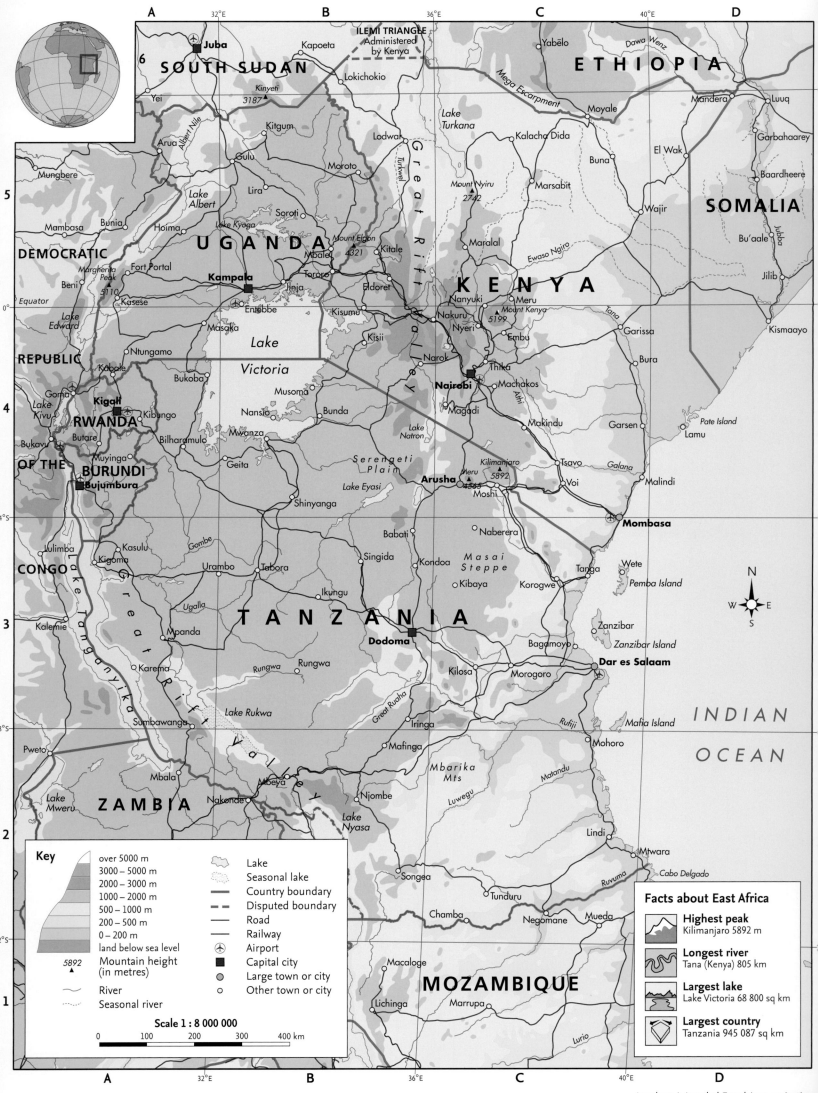

SOUTH SUDAN

ETHIOPIA

Juba
Kapoeta
Yabēlo
Dawa Wenz

Yei
Kinyeti
3187
Lokichokio
Mandera
Luuq

Mega Escarpment

Kitgum
Lodwar
Moyale
Garbahaarey

Arua
Gulu
Lake
Turkana
Kalacha Dida

Albert Nile

Mungbere
Lira
Turkwel
El Wak
Baardheere

Mambasa
Bunia
Soroti
Mount Nyiru
2742
Marsabit
Buna
Wajir
SOMALIA

Hoima
Lake Kyoga
Mbale
Mount Elgon
4321
Kitale
Maralal
Bu'aale
Jubba

DEMOCRATIC

UGANDA

Fort Portal
Kampala
Jinja
Tororo
Eldoret
Nanyuki
Meru

Margherita
Peak
5110
Kasese
Entebbe
Kisumu
Nakuru
Mount Kenya
5199
Embu
Garissa

Beni
Equator
Masaka
Kisii
Nyeri
Tana
Jilib

REPUBLIC
Lake
Edward
Ntungamo
Lake
Victoria
Narok
Nairobi
Machakos
Bura
Kismaayo

Kabale
Bukoba
Musoma
Thika
Athi
Pate Island

Goma
Kigali
Kibungo
Nansio
Bunda
Magadi
Makindu
Garsen
Lamu

Lake
Kivu
RWANDA
Bilharamulo
Mwanza
Lake
Natron
Kilimanjaro
5892
Tsavo
Galana
Malindi

Bukavu
Butare
Muyinga
Geita
Serengeti
Plain
Meru
4565
Moshi
Voi

OF THE
BURUNDI
Bujumbura
Lake Eyasi
Arusha

Shinyanga
Naberera
Mombasa

CONGO
Lulimba
Kasulu
Gombe
Babati
Masai
Steppe
Wete
Pemba Island

Kigoma
Urambo
Tabora
Singida
Kondoa
Kibaya
Korogwe
Tanga

Ugalla
Ikungu
Zanzibar
Zanzibar Island

Kalemie
Mpanda
TANZANIA
Dodoma
Bagamoyo

Lake Tanganyika
Karema
Rungwa
Rungwa
Kilosa
Morogoro
Dar es Salaam

Great Rift Valley
Great Ruaha
Rufiji
Mafia Island
INDIAN

Sumbawanga
Lake Rukwa
Iringa
OCEAN

Pweto
Mafinga
Mohoro

Mbala
Mbeya
Njombe
Mbarika
Mts
Matandu

ZAMBIA
Nakonde
Luwegu
Lindi

Lake
Mweru
Lake
Nyasa
Mtwara

Cabo Delgado

Songea
Ruvuma

Tunduru
Mueda

Chamba
Negomane

Macaloge
MOZAMBIQUE

Lichinga
Marrupa
Lurio

Key

over 5000 m	
3000 – 5000 m	
2000 – 3000 m	
1000 – 2000 m	
500 – 1000 m	
200 – 500 m	
0 – 200 m	

land below sea level

5892 ▲ Mountain height (in metres)

River

Seasonal river

Lake

Seasonal lake

Country boundary

Disputed boundary

Road

Railway

✈ Airport

■ Capital city

⬤ Large town or city

○ Other town or city

Scale 1 : 8 000 000

0   100   200   300   400 km

Facts about East Africa

Highest peak
Kilimanjaro 5892 m

Longest river
Tana (Kenya) 805 km

Largest lake
Lake Victoria 68 800 sq km

Largest country
Tanzania 945 087 sq km

Lambert Azimuthal Equal Area projection

Annual rainfall

The heaviest rain falls in April and May. The highlands and western areas receive ample rainfall but most of the north and northeast is very dry.

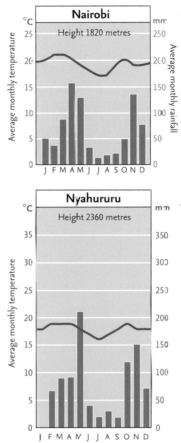

Average annual rainfall

- more than 2000 mm
- 1000 – 2000 mm
- 500 – 1000 mm
- less than 500 mm

Scale 1 : 12 000 000

@ National Bureau of Statistics
www.knbs.or.ke
World Meteorological Organization
www.wmo.int

Climate graphs

Kenya has a tropical climate which varies with altitude. The coastal lowland area is hot and humid but the highlands region is much drier and cooler.

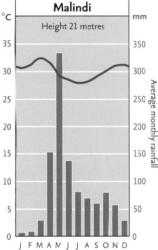

Malindi on the east coast enjoys temperatures around 30 °C all year round. Nyahururu, the highest town in Kenya, and Nairobi have temperatures around 20 °C all year. The wettest month is April in Nairobi and May in Nyahururu and Malindi.

Vegetation

Large areas of Kenya are covered in sparsely wooded savanna. The most varied vegetation is found in the highlands where savanna gives way to woodland and forest. North of the river Tana semi desert areas support little vegetation.

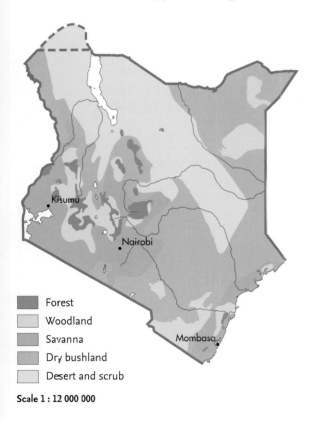

- Forest
- Woodland
- Savanna
- Dry bushland
- Desert and scrub

Scale 1 : 12 000 000

Population

Kenya's population is distributed very unevenly. The most densely populated areas are found in areas with adequate rainfall. The main urban settlements are Nairobi and Mombasa. The dry north and northeast areas are sparsely populated as lack of water limits the development of any settlement.

Persons per sq km
- over 100
- 50 – 100
- 10 – 50
- 1 – 10
- 0 – 1

Cities and towns
- ● over 1 000 000
- ● 100 000 – 1 000 000
- · 25 000 – 100 000
- — Selected former administrative boundaries

The former Central region is more densely populated than the former Coast region. The population in both historical regions has grown steadily since 1960.

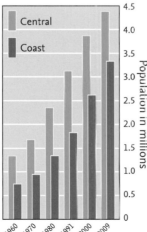

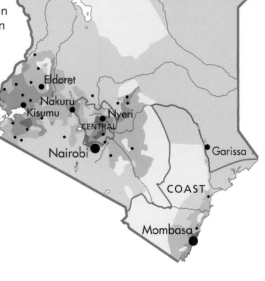

Scale 1 : 12 000 000

Tourism

Tourism makes an important contribution to Kenya's economy. The main attractions are wildlife in the National Parks and National Reserves, and the resorts on the Indian Ocean coast. The temperature is over 20 °C throughout the country all year.

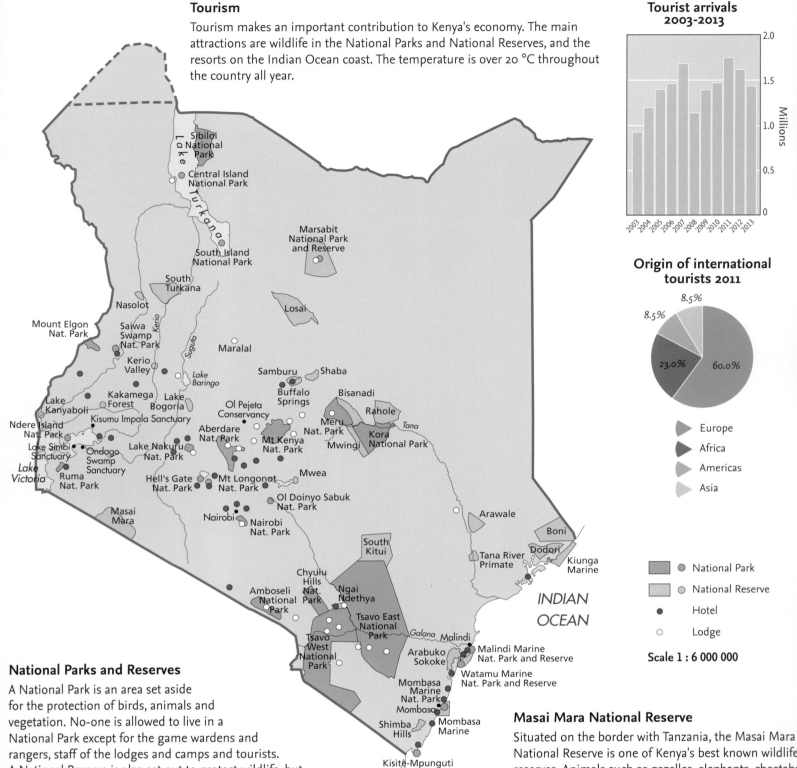

Tourist arrivals 2003-2013

(Bar chart showing tourist arrivals in Millions, vertical axis 0 to 2.0, horizontal axis years 2003, 2004, 2005, 2006, 2007, 2008, 2009, 2010, 2011, 2012, 2013)

Origin of international tourists 2011

(Pie chart)
- 60.0%
- 23.0%
- 8.5%
- 8.5%

- Europe
- Africa
- Americas
- Asia

Legend:
- National Park (shaded area with ● symbol)
- National Reserve (shaded area with ○ symbol)
- ● Hotel
- ○ Lodge

Scale 1 : 6 000 000

(Map of Kenya with labels: Sibiloi National Park, Central Island National Park, South Island National Park, Lake Turkana, Marsabit National Park and Reserve, South Turkana, Losai, Nasolot, Mount Elgon Nat. Park, Saiwa Swamp Nat. Park, Kerio, Suguta, Maralal, Kerio Valley, Lake Baringo, Samburu, Shaba, Kakamega Forest, Lake Bogoria, Buffalo Springs, Bisanadi, Rahole, Ol Pejeta Conservancy, Meru Nat. Park, Kora National Park, Mwingi, Tana, Lake Kanyaboli, Kisumu Impala Sanctuary, Aberdare Nat. Park, Mt Kenya Nat. Park, Ndere Island Nat. Park, Lake Simbi Sanctuary, Ondago Swamp Sanctuary, Lake Nakuru Nat. Park, Mwea, Lake Victoria, Ruma Nat. Park, Hell's Gate Nat. Park, Mt Longonot Nat. Park, Ol Doinyo Sabuk Nat. Park, Masai Mara, Nairobi, Nairobi Nat. Park, Arawale, Boni, South Kitui, Dodori, Tana River Primate, Kiunga Marine, Chyulu Hills Nat. Park, Ngai Ndethya, Amboseli National Park, Tsavo East National Park, Galana, Malindi, Tsavo West National Park, Arabuko Sokoke, Malindi Marine Nat. Park and Reserve, Watamu Marine Nat. Park and Reserve, Mombasa Marine Nat. Park, Mombasa, Mombasa Marine, Shimba Hills, Kisite-Mpunguti Marine Park and Reserve, INDIAN OCEAN)

National Parks and Reserves

A National Park is an area set aside for the protection of birds, animals and vegetation. No-one is allowed to live in a National Park except for the game wardens and rangers, staff of the lodges and camps and tourists. A National Reserve is also set out to protect wildlife, but local people can live and keep their cattle in the reserve.

Masai Mara National Reserve

Situated on the border with Tanzania, the Masai Mara National Reserve is one of Kenya's best known wildlife reserves. Animals such as gazelles, elephants, cheetahs, buffalo and a few black rhino live here all year round.

Endangered species - Rhinos

Since 1980 the Rhino population has declined, due mainly to hunting. Sanctuaries such as the Ol Pejeta Conservancy are dedicated to the conservation of the Black Rhino. By 2010 the population increased to 630.

Black Rhino population

1980	1987	1993	2003	2005	2010	2015
1500	521	417	428	539	630	620

@ **Kenya Tourist Board**
www.magicalkenya.com
The Africa Guide
www.africaguide.com

For four months every year herds of wildebeest from Tanzania graze on the Mara plains. Tall grasses are reduced to stubble before the herds trek south again.

Threats to the natural environment in East Africa include deforestation, soil erosion, desertification, water shortage and water pollution. Forest output has declined due to over exploitation and soil erosion has resulted in the silting of dams and the loss of biodiversity.

The three case studies below outline some of the current environmental problems faced in East African countries.

Maathai Wangari

In the 1970s, the Green Belt Movement, founded by Maathai Wangari, focused on the planting of trees and environmental conservation. Over the years 30 million seedling trees have been planted in an effort to protect the environment and the habitats of endangered wildlife.

Kenya
Nanyuki River in Central Kenya

Issue The Nanyuki river has become shallow and the water is stagnant and dirty.
Local residents rely on river water for domestic use, livestock and farming.

Causes Large scale removal of forest from the river banks and surrounding hills mainly for fuel.

Effect Evaporation of the river water.

Action **River Management**
- Reforestation is essential.
- Local people need to be encouraged to plant more trees.
- Businesses need to be re-located further from the river to reduce pollution of its waters.
- Irrigation needs to be controlled.

On-going concerns
- There is a lack of alternative sources of fuel.
- Climate change has resulted in a loss of snow and ice on the mountain tops.

Uganda
Co-operative farming of organic cotton in Northern Uganda

Issue Degradation of soils in Northern Uganda.

Cause Mis-management of land and poor farming practices.

Action
- Investment by international organisation in organic cotton farming.
- Introduction of crop rotation to include food crops.
- Use of organic pesticides.

Result
- High yield of organic cotton crops.
- Increase in production of food crops such as millet, maize and beans.
- Re-vitalisation of local economy.
- Northern Uganda is now a hub for cotton growing.
- About 24 000 farmers are now growing organic cotton in Lira District.

Tanzania
Receding icecap of Kilimanjaro

These two images illustrate the changes over time in snow cover at the summit of Kilimanjaro. Ice on the summit has shrunk gradually over the past century. Most scientists forecast that the glaciers of Kilimanjaro will be gone by the year 2060. This could be due to climate change and climatologists are currently studying weather trends and environmental changes.

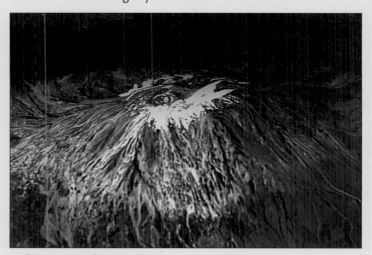

The loss of Kilimanjaro's permanent icecap will impact on local populations who depend on access to melt water from the ice fields for fresh water during dry seasons and monsoon failures.

Ice fields on top of Kilimanjaro 1993

Ice fields on top of Kilimanjaro 2000

Key

over 5000 m
3000 – 5000 m
2000 – 3000 m
1000 – 2000 m
500 – 1000 m
200 – 500 m
0 – 200 m
land below sea level

Ice cap

6190 ▲ Mountain height (in metres)

Scale 1 : 40 000 000

0   500   1000   1500 km

Facts about North America

Area
24 680 331 sq km

Highest peak
Denali 6190 m

Lowest point
Death Valley -86 m

Longest river
Mississippi-Missouri 5969 km

Largest lake
Lake Superior 82 100 sq km

Lambert Azimuthal Equal Area projection

This is a false colour image of North and Central America and Greenland. The different colours have been chosen to highlight the many different environments of the region. The cold areas, often with permanent snow and ice, are shown in pale grey. The frozen sea ice of the Arctic Ocean is grey-green. The tundra areas are shown in yellow. The prairies are highlighted in brownish reds and the dark reds show areas of rich grasslands and deciduous forest.

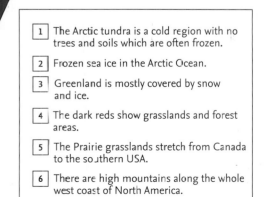

1. The Arctic tundra is a cold region with no trees and soils which are often frozen.

2. Frozen sea ice in the Arctic Ocean.

3. Greenland is mostly covered by snow and ice.

4. The dark reds show grasslands and forest areas.

5. The Prairie grasslands stretch from Canada to the southern USA.

6. There are high mountains along the whole west coast of North America.

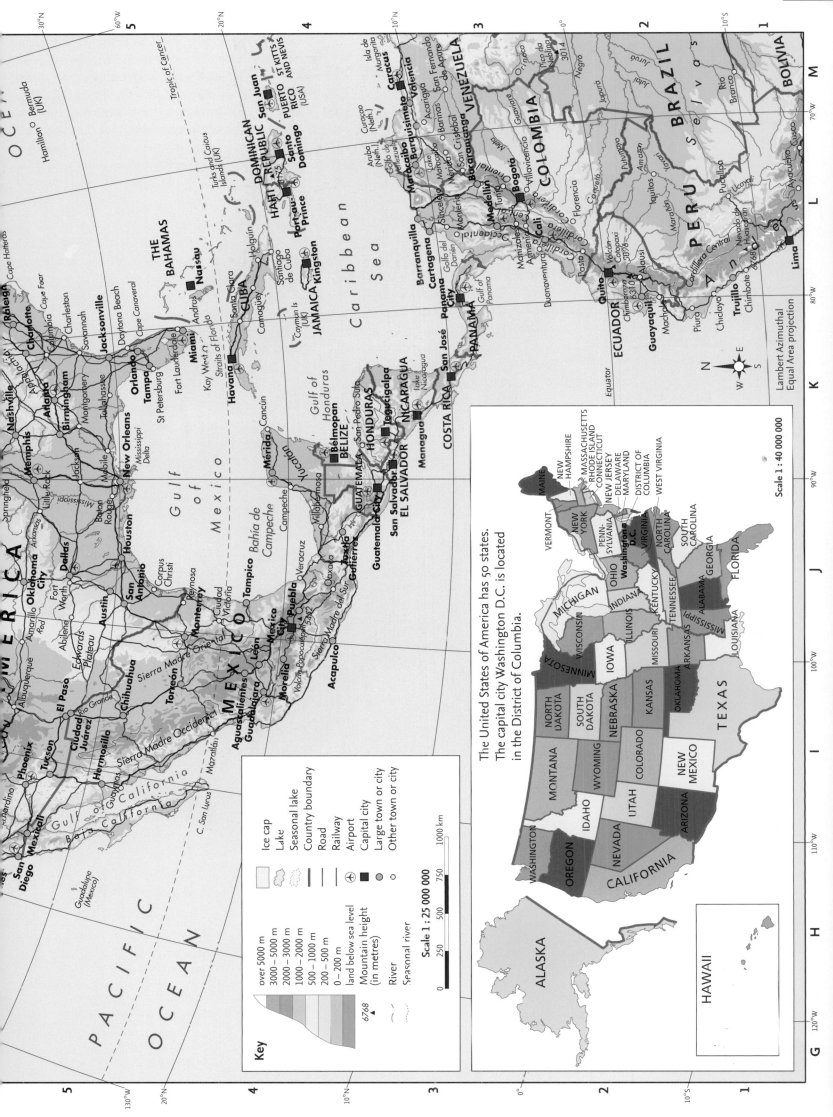

This image of the San Francisco Bay area was photographed from the International Space Station. The grey urban areas contrast with the green hillsides. Pink areas at the southeast of the bay are salt marshes. Tidal channels can be clearly seen within the bay and the outflow of bay water creates a plume as it travels towards the Pacific Ocean.

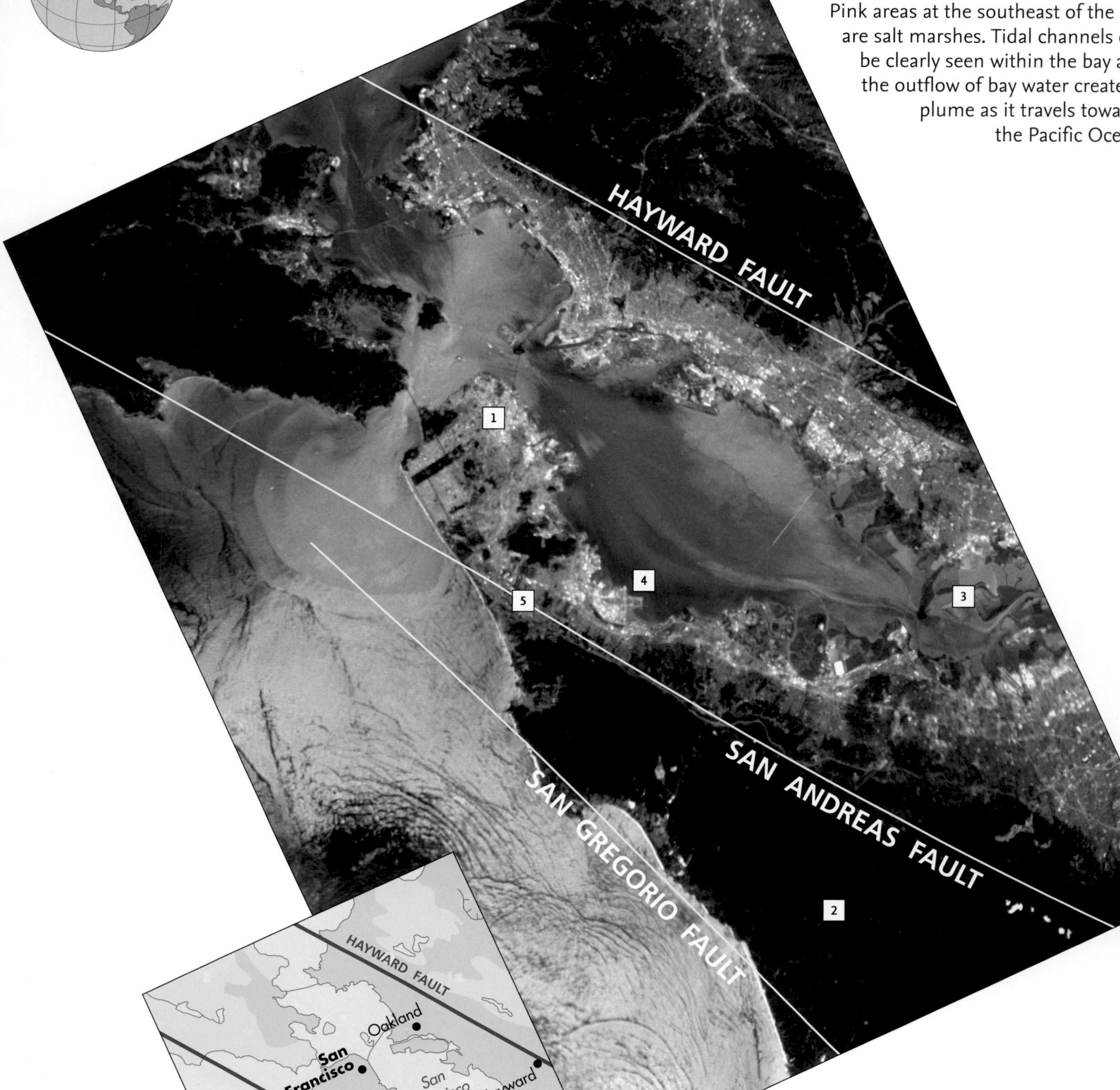

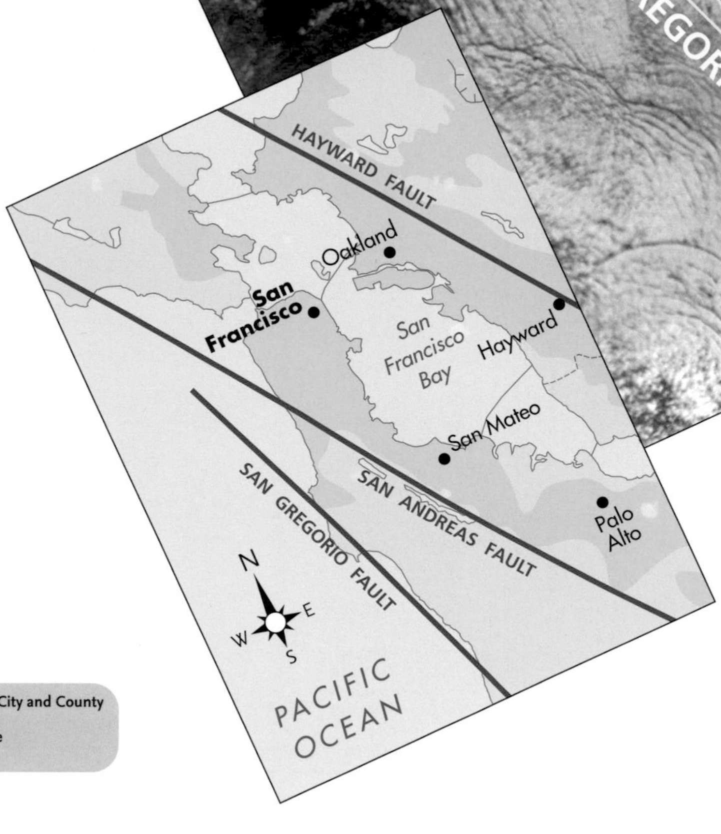

HAYWARD FAULT

SAN ANDREAS FAULT

SAN GREGORIO FAULT

HAYWARD FAULT

Oakland

San Francisco

San Francisco Bay

Hayward

San Mateo

SAN ANDREAS FAULT

SAN GREGORIO FAULT

Palo Alto

N E S W

PACIFIC OCEAN

@ San Francisco City and County
www.sfgov.org
California State
www.ca.gov

1. The built-up area surrounds San Francisco Bay.
2. Areas of dense woodland cover much of the Santa Cruz Mountains.
3. Marshland and salt marshes.
4. San Francisco International Airport juts out into the bay.
5. Main fault line.

This is a natural colour image showing Hurricane Katrina striking the Gulf Coast of the USA on 28 August 2005. The hurricane, an enormous rotating storm, appears clearly as a white swirl of cloud. Winds are strongest in the centre of the swirl where they reached 257 kph. The green areas are land and the dark blue-black areas are the waters of the Gulf of Mexico.

1	The eye or centre of the hurricane
2	Gulf of Mexico
3	Mississippi Delta
4	Cuba
5	USA
6	Mexico

@ National Hurricane Center
www.nhc.noaa.gov
National Oceanic and Atmospheric Administration
www.noaa.gov

Hurricane tracks

Hurricanes originate in the warm, moist tropical air over the Atlantic Ocean and move westwards at about 20 kph. Their power declines rapidly as they pass over land or cooler water and they usually last for about 9 days.

Hurricane risk

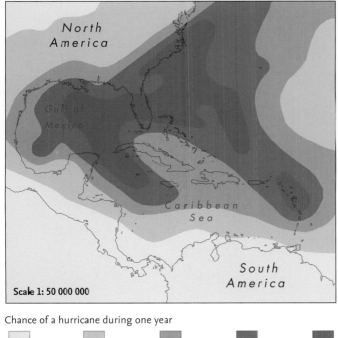

Scale 1: 50 000 000

Chance of a hurricane during one year

less than 5%	5 – 35%	35 – 55%	55 – 65%	65 – 90%

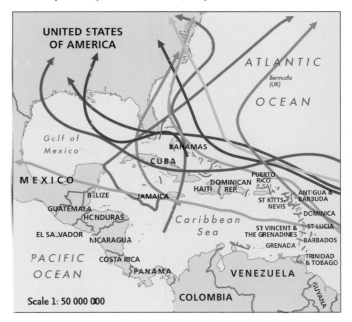

Scale 1: 50 000 000

Tracks of major hurricanes from 1990

Andrew 1992	Charley 2004	Ike 2008
Fran 1996	Katrina 2005	Sandy 2012
Floyd 1999	Wilma 2005	Gonzalo 2014
Isabel 2003	Dean 2007	

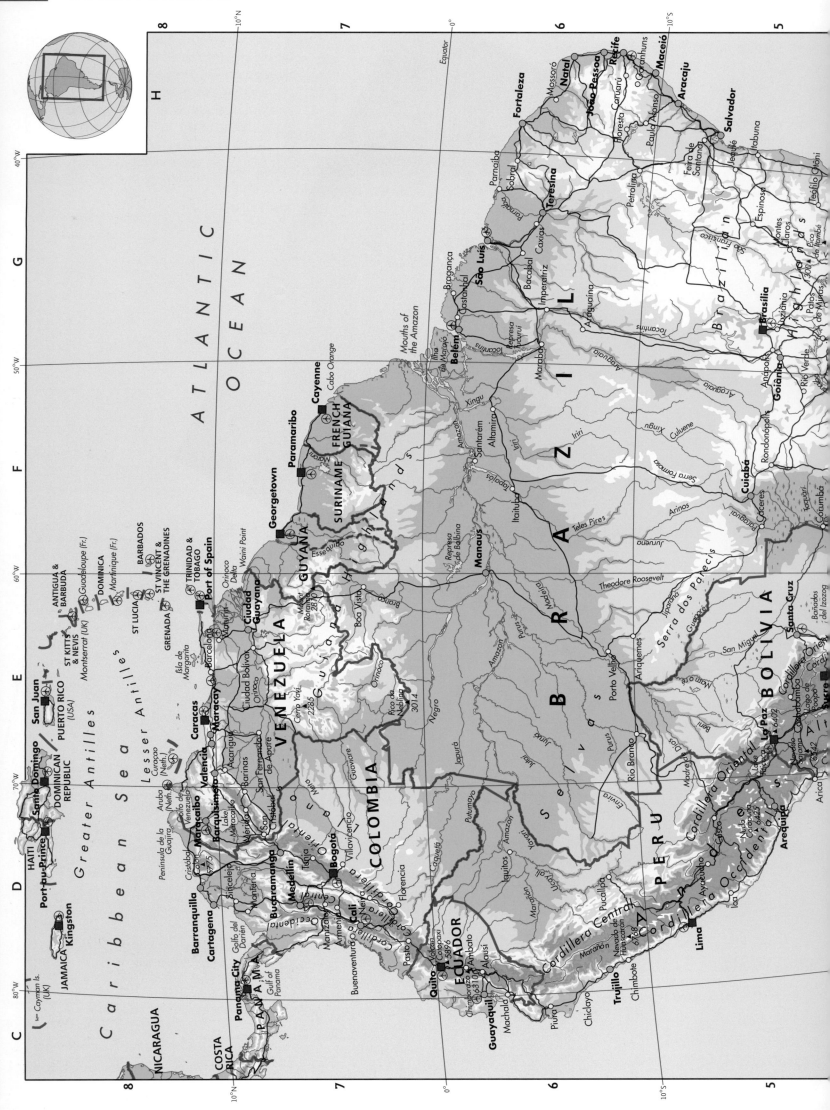

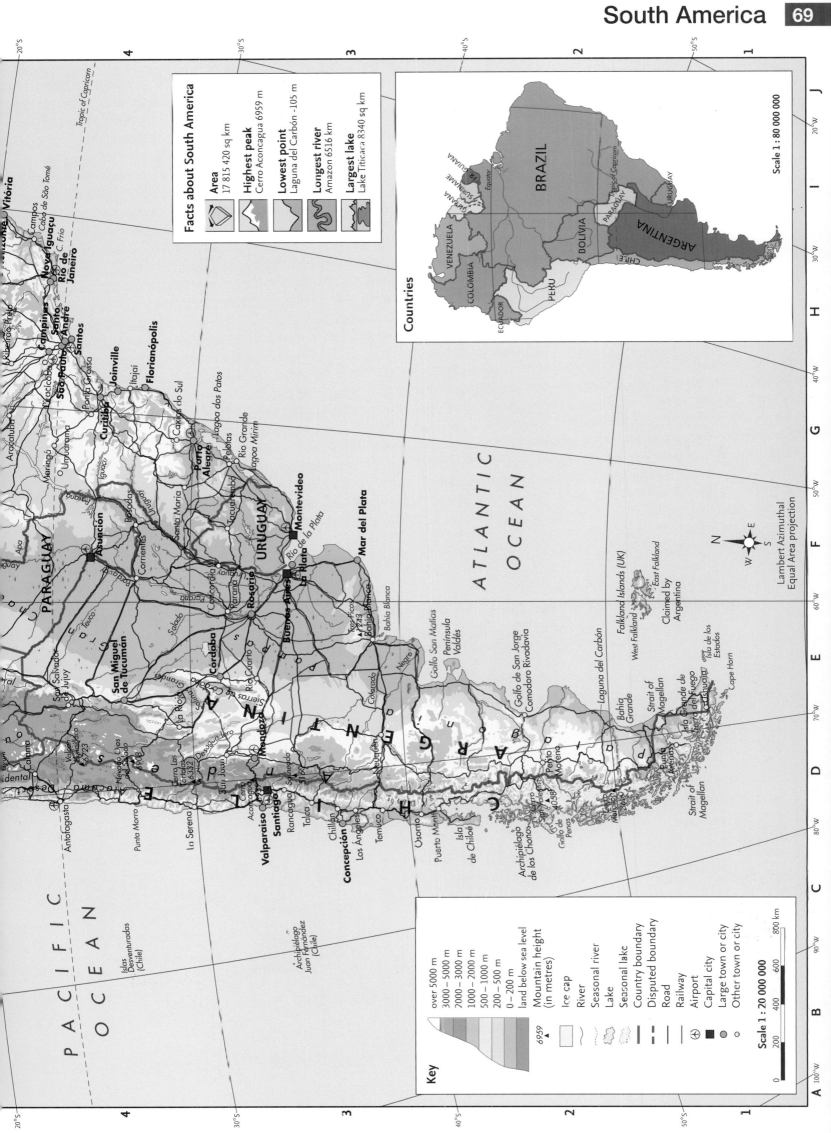

COLOMBIA

8

RORAIMA

GUYANA

Serra Tumucumaque

AMAPÁ

Boa Vista

Pico da
Neblina
3014

Represa
de Balbina

Macapá

Mouths of the
Amazon

Cabo
Maguarinho

Ilha de Maracá

Bragança

Ilha de
Marajó

Belém

Castar

A M A Z O N A S

Manaus

Santarém

Amazon

Xingu

PARÁ

Altamira

Iquitos

Itaituba

Tapajós

Marabá

Imperatri

PERU

Pucallpa

ACRE

Porto Velho

Rio Branco

Riberalta

Ariquemes

RONDÔNIA

Serra da Parecís

MATO GROSSO

B R A Z I L

TOCANTINS

Araguaína

Tocantins

Huancayo

Ayacucho

Cusco

Cordillera Oriental

Madre de Dios

Serra Formosa

Xingu

Represa
Tucuruí

Nudo
Coropuna
6425

Cordillera Occidental

Arequipa

La Paz

Lake
Titicaca

Cochabamba

Nevado
Sajama
6542

Oruro

Lago de
Poopó

B O L I V I A

Yungas

Cordillera Oriental

Cordillera Central

Santa
Cruz

Bañados
del Izozóg

Cáceres

Cuiabá

Cuiabá

Rondonópolis

Pantanal

Lagoa
Mandioré

Taquarí

Corumbá

MATO GROSSO

Brazilian

DISTRITO
FEDERAL

Brasília

GOIÁS

Goiânia

Anápolis

Luziânia

Highlands

Rio
Verde

Araguari

Uberlândia

Uberaba

Patos
de Min

Arica

Sucre

Potosí

Salar
de Uyuni

Iquique

CHILE

Tocopilla

PACIFIC

OCEAN

Paraguay

San Miguel

DO SUL

Campo
Grande

Dourados

Pardo

Presidente
Prudente

Araçatuba

Barretos

Franca

Ribeirão Pr

SÃO
PAULO

Bauru

Piracicaba

Camp

São Carlos

San

Sant

P A R A G U A Y

San Salvador
de Jujuy

Teuco

Pilcomayo

Paraná

Maringá

Apucarana

São Paulo

Sorocaba

Sant

Salta

Asunción

P A R A N Á

Ponta Grossa

Paranapiacaba

A R G E N T I N A

San Miguel
de Tucumán

Formosa

Paraguay

Posadas

Iguaçu
Falls

Iguaçu

Guarapuava

Chapecó

Curitiba

Joinville

Itajaí

SANTA
CATARINA

Florianópolis

Resistencia

Corrientes

Uruguay

Corrientes

Passo
Fundo

Serra do Mar

La Rioja

Patquía

Salinas
Grandes

Salado

RIO GRANDE

Caxias do Sul

Nova Hamburgo

Uruguaiana

Santa
Maria

Santa Cruz
do Sul

Canoas

Porto Alegre

DO SUL

Córdoba

Santa
Fé

Concordia

Paraná

Pelotas

Lagoa
dos Patos

Sierras de Córdoba

Champaquí
2880

Rosario

Paraná

U R U G U A Y

Tacuarembó

Rio Grande

Lagoa Mirim

Río Cuarto

Río
Uruguay

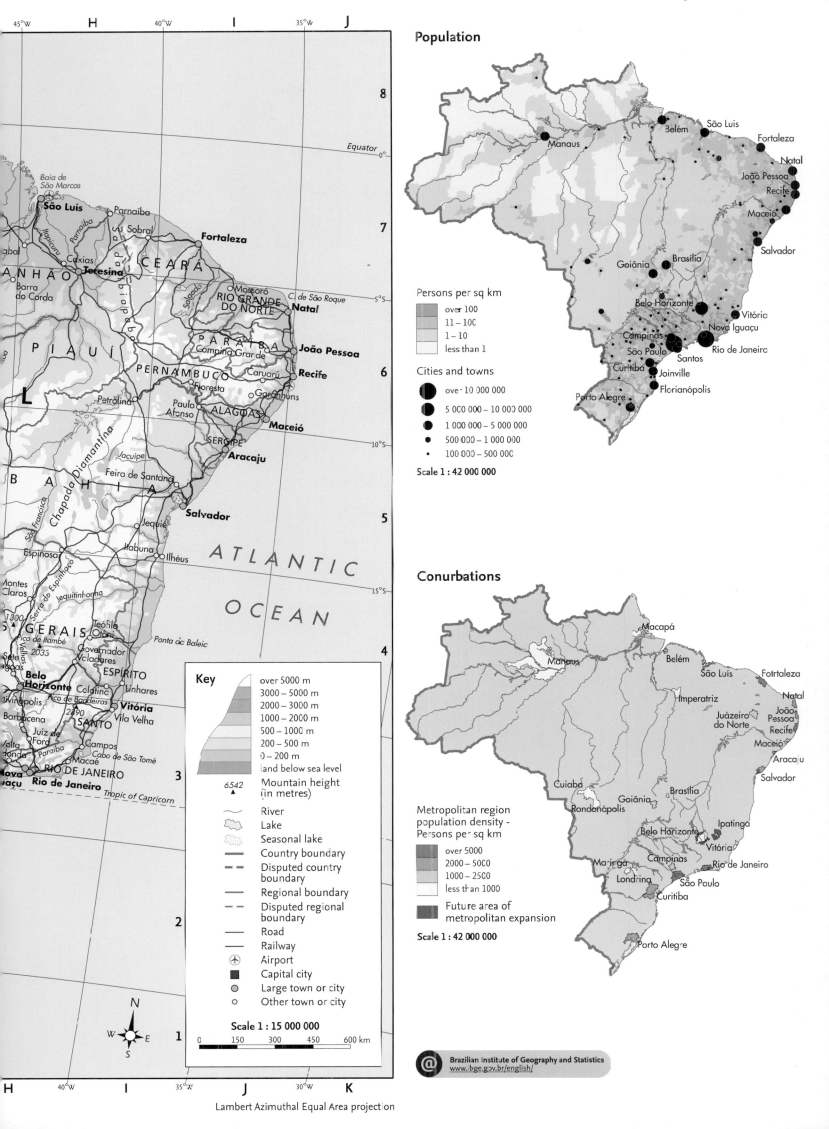

Annual rainfall

Average annual rainfall

- more than 2400 mm
- 2000 – 2400 mm
- 1600 – 2000 mm
- 1200 – 1600 mm
- 800 – 1200 mm
- less than 800 mm

Scale 1 : 60 000 000

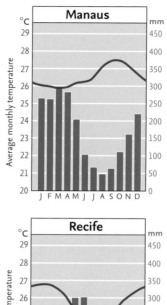

Rain falls throughout Brazil all year round. The Amazon Basin receives most rain and Belém is one of the wettest cities in the world.

@ World Meteorological Organization
www.wmo.ch

Climate graphs and statistics

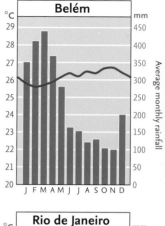

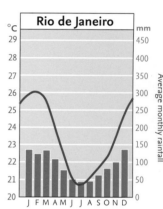

Temperature: January

Average temperature

- over 25 °C
- 20 – 25 °C
- 15 – 20 °C
- 10 – 15 °C

→ Wind direction

Scale 1 : 60 000 000

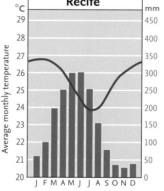

Summer lasts from December to February. Temperatures are usually over 30 °C. The south is hot and humid. The northeast is drier with fresh tropical breezes.

Manaus	Jan	Feb	Mar	Apr	May	Jun	Jul	Aug	Sep	Oct	Nov	Dec
Temperature - °C	26.0	26.0	25.9	26.0	26.2	26.3	26.5	27.2	27.5	27.5	27.1	26.6
Rainfall - mm	264	262	298	283	204	103	67	46	63	111	161	220

Belém	Jan	Feb	Mar	Apr	May	Jun	Jul	Aug	Sep	Oct	Nov	Dec
Temperature - °C	25.8	25.6	25.7	25.9	26.1	26.4	26.2	26.5	26.4	26.7	26.7	26.4
Rainfall - mm	351	412	441	370	282	164	154	122	129	105	101	202

Recife	Jan	Feb	Mar	Apr	May	Jun	Jul	Aug	Sep	Oct	Nov	Dec
Temperature - °C	26.8	26.8	26.6	26.1	25.3	24.5	23.9	23.9	24.7	25.6	26.1	26.5
Rainfall - mm	62	102	197	252	301	302	254	156	78	36	29	40

Rio de Janeiro	Jan	Feb	Mar	Apr	May	Jun	Jul	Aug	Sep	Oct	Nov	Dec
Temperature - °C	26.0	26.2	25.6	24.1	22.4	21.1	20.7	21.2	21.6	22.3	23.4	24.9
Rainfall - mm	135	124	134	109	78	52	45	46	62	82	100	137

Temperature: July

Average temperature

- over 25 °C
- 20 – 25 °C
- 15 – 20 °C
- 10 – 15 °C

→ Wind direction

Scale 1 : 60 000 000

Winter in Brazil lasts from June to August. It is only in the southern states that temperatures fall below 20 °C. The rest of the country has moderate temperatures.

Climate zones

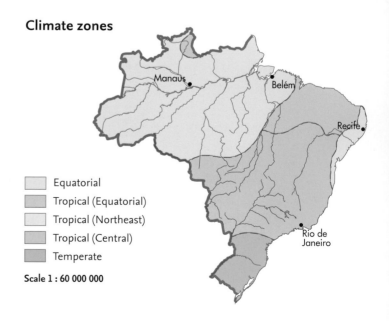

- Equatorial
- Tropical (Equatorial)
- Tropical (Northeast)
- Tropical (Central)
- Temperate

Scale 1 : 60 000 000

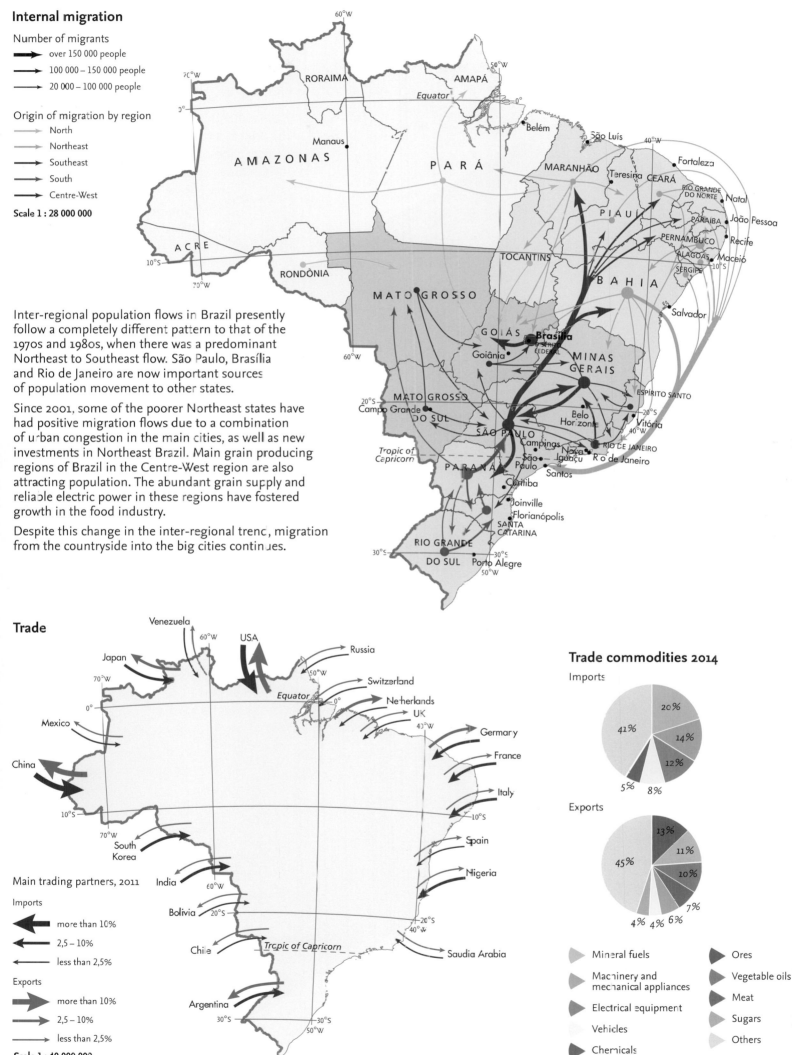

Internal migration

Number of migrants

→ over 150 000 people
→ 100 000 – 150 000 people
→ 20 000 – 100 000 people

Origin of migration by region

→ North
→ Northeast
→ Southeast
→ South
→ Centre-West

Scale 1 : 28 000 000

Inter-regional population flows in Brazil presently follow a completely different pattern to that of the 1970s and 1980s, when there was a predominant Northeast to Southeast flow. São Paulo, Brasília and Rio de Janeiro are now important sources of population movement to other states.

Since 2001, some of the poorer Northeast states have had positive migration flows due to a combination of urban congestion in the main cities, as well as new investments in Northeast Brazil. Main grain producing regions of Brazil in the Centre-West region are also attracting population. The abundant grain supply and reliable electric power in these regions have fostered growth in the food industry.

Despite this change in the inter-regional trend, migration from the countryside into the big cities continues.

Trade

Main trading partners, 2011

Imports

← more than 10%
← 2,5 – 10%
← less than 2,5%

Exports

→ more than 10%
→ 2,5 – 10%
→ less than 2,5%

Scale 1 : 40 000 000

Trade commodities 2014

Imports

- 41%
- 20%
- 14%
- 12%
- 8%
- 5%

Exports

- 45%
- 13%
- 11%
- 10%
- 7%
- 6%
- 4%
- 4%

- Mineral fuels
- Machinery and mechanical appliances
- Electrical equipment
- Vehicles
- Chemicals
- Ores
- Vegetable oils
- Meat
- Sugars
- Others

This is a true colour image of part of the Amazon rainforest. The Madeira river is a tributary of the Amazon and flows across the top left of the image. The straight lines in the forest show where whole blocks of trees have been cut down. Smoke plumes from forest fires is evidence that slash and burn farming is still being practised in the forest.

1	Areas where the rainforest has not yet been cut down.
2	Deforested areas of land cleared for commercial logging.
3	Smoke plumes from forest fires.
4	Madeira river flowing through the forest.

Amazonia: Development

The largest tropical rainforest in the world is in Amazonia in Brazil. Most deforestation has taken place on the edges of the forest in the east, south and southwest. Satellite images like the one opposite allow the Brazilian government to monitor damage to the forest and take steps to prevent unnecessary exploitation of the forest.

☐ Location of satellite image shown on page 74

HEP developments (>100MW)
- ▬ HEP Dam
- ▬ HEP Dam (planned)

Communications
- ——— Railway
- ----- Railway (planned)
- ——— Road
- ----- Road (planned)

Land Use
- ☐ Cropland and woodland
- ☐ Grassland and grazing
- ☐ Grassland and woodland
- ☐ Tropical forest
- ☐ Temperate forest
- ☐ Scrubland or desert
- ☐ Swamp or marsh
- ☐ Deforestation
- ——— Extent of Amazonia in Brazil

Scale 1 : 30 000 000

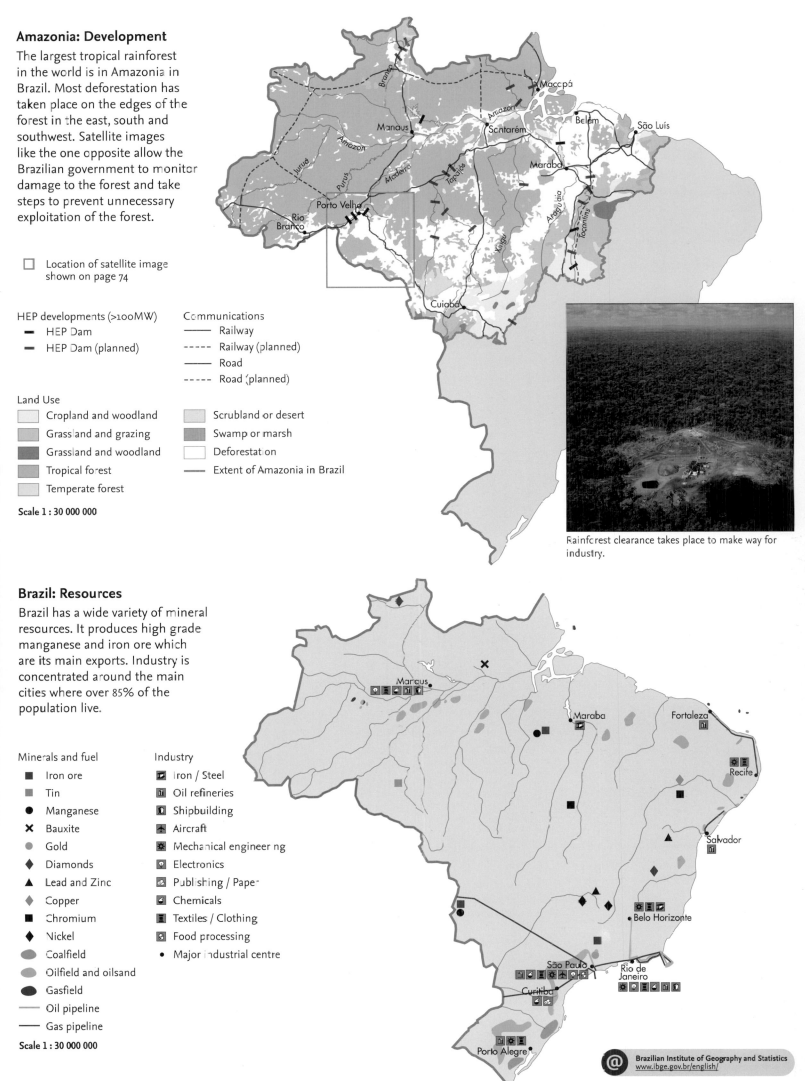

Rainforest clearance takes place to make way for industry.

Brazil: Resources

Brazil has a wide variety of mineral resources. It produces high grade manganese and iron ore which are its main exports. Industry is concentrated around the main cities where over 85% of the population live.

Minerals and fuel
- ■ Iron ore
- ■ Tin
- ● Manganese
- ✕ Bauxite
- ● Gold
- ◆ Diamonds
- ▲ Lead and Zinc
- ◆ Copper
- ■ Chromium
- ◆ Nickel
- ⬤ Coalfield
- ⬤ Oilfield and oilsand
- ⬤ Gasfield
- ——— Oil pipeline
- ——— Gas pipeline

Scale 1 : 30 000 000

Industry
- 🏭 Iron / Steel
- 🏢 Oil refineries
- 🚢 Shipbuilding
- ✈ Aircraft
- ✳ Mechanical engineering
- 🖥 Electronics
- ✎ Publishing / Paper
- ◧ Chemicals
- 📚 Textiles / Clothing
- 🍴 Food processing
- ● Major industrial centre

@ **Brazilian Institute of Geography and Statistics**
www.ibge.gov.br/english/

Key

- over 5000 m
- 3000 – 5000 m
- 2000 – 3000 m
- 1000 – 2000 m
- 500 – 1000 m
- 200 – 500 m
- 0 – 200 m
- land below sea level
- ▲ 4884 Mountain height (in metres)
- River
- Seasonal river
- Lake
- Seasonal lake
- Country boundary
- Regional boundary
- Road
- Railway
- Airport
- ■ Capital city
- ● Large town or city
- ○ Other town or city

Scale 1 : 20 000 000

0   200   400   600   800 km

Facts about Australia, New Zealand and Southwest Pacific

Population
39 331 000

Largest city
Sydney 4 844 000

Largest country
Australia 7 692 024 sq km

Country with most people
Australia 23 969 000

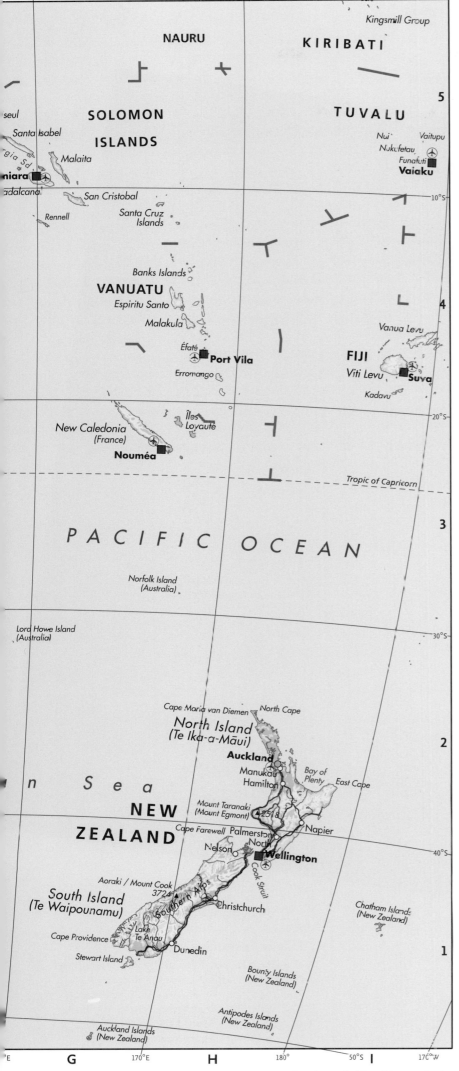

Lambert Azimuthal Equal Area projection

Bushfires

In Australia bushfires are a serious hazard in the dry season especially in the southeast and southwest of the continent.

Bushfire in Central Arnhem Land

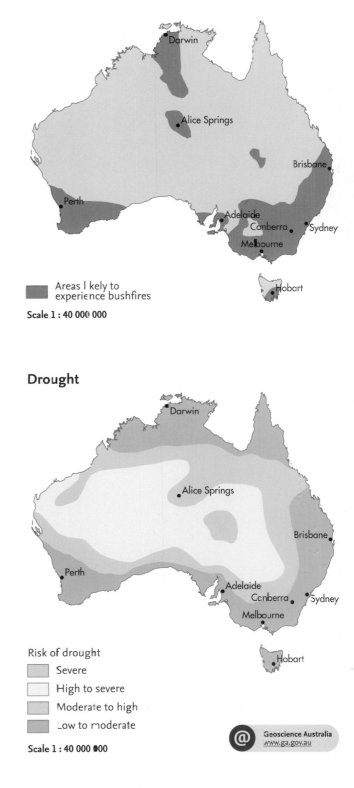

Areas likely to experience bushfires

Scale 1 : 40 000 000

Drought

Risk of drought

Severe

High to severe

Moderate to high

Low to moderate

Scale 1 : 40 000 000

This is a simulated natural colour image of Australia, New Zealand and the nearby parts of southeast Asia and the southwest Pacific Ocean. The desert of central and western Australia is shown in pink-brown, whilst the greens on the image show those areas with forests and farmland. Areas of grassland are shown in grey-green.

Visible Earth
visibleearth.nasa.gov
MODIS web imagery
modis.gsfc.nasa.gov

1   The centre of Australia is a hot desert. You can see some mountain ranges in the western areas.

2   Southeast Australia is one of the main farming areas of the country as the green colours show.

3   The island of Tasmania is covered by grassland, forest and farmland.

4   Because New Zealand is further south than Australia it is cooler and wetter. As a result there are more forests.

Fragile Environment

The Great Barrier Reef, along the Queensland coast, is the largest barrier reef in the world. The impact of over-fishing, pollution, coral bleaching and in sea temperature rise due to global warming requires action to protect and preserve this unique environment.

Annual rainfall

Average annual rainfall

- 1000 – 2000 mm
- 500 – 1000 mm
- 250 – 500 mm
- less than 250 mm

Scale 1 : 60 000 000

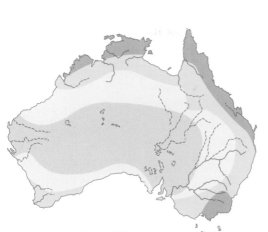

Australia is the driest continent and rainfall is highly variable across the country. The wettest areas are northeast Queensland and southwest Tasmania; the centre of Australia is hot and dry.

Temperature: January

Average temperature

- over 32 °C
- 24 – 32 °C
- 16 – 24 °C
- 8 – 16 °C

→ Wind direction

Scale 1 : 60 000 000

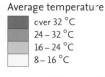

Summer lasts from December to February. In January average temperatures exceed 30 °C. The hottest areas are northwest Western Australia and from southwest Queensland across south Australia into southeast Western Australia.

@ World Meteorological Organization
www.wmo.ch
Australian Bureau of Statistics
www.abs.gov.au

Temperature: July

Average temperature

- over 24 °C
- 16 – 24 °C
- 8 – 16 °C
- 0 – 3 °C
- below 0 °C

→ Wind direction

Scale 1 : 60 000 000

Winter lasts from June to August. The lowest average temperature is between 7 °C in the northwest and 5 °C in the southeast. Snow is confined to the mountainous regions of the southeast.

Population

Persons per sq km

- over 50
- 10 – 50
- 1 – 10
- 0 – 1

Cities and towns

- ● 2 500 000 – 5 000 000
- • 1 000 000 – 2 500 000

Scale 1 : 60 000 000

Australia has one of the lowest population densities in the world. Distribution is uneven with most people living along the eastern and south eastern coasts. The main urban areas are Adelaide, Brisbane, Melbourne, Perth and Sydney.

Sydney

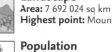

Space Imaging

Sydney is Australia's largest city with a population of 4 844 000.

Facts about Australia

Landscape
Area: 7 692 024 sq km
Highest point: Mount Kosciuszko 2229 m

Population
Total: 23 969 000
Density: 3 persons per sq km

Settlement
% Urban population: 89
Main towns/cities: Sydney, Melbourne, Adelaide, Brisbane, Perth

Land use
Main crops: Wheat, sugar, rice, barley
Main industries: Food products, chemicals, transport equipment

Development indicators
Life expectancy: male 80, female 84
GNI per capita: US$ 64 680
Primary school enrolment ratio: 97
% Access to safe water: 100

Manned bases in the Antarctic Peninsula

① Frei (Chile)
② Comandante Ferraz (Brazil)
③ Bellingshausen (Russia)
④ Carlini (Argentina)
⑤ Arctowski (Poland)
⑥ Bernardo O'Higgins (Chile)
⑦ Great Wall (China)
⑧ Artigas (Uruguay)
⑨ Escudero (Chile)
⑩ San Martin (Argentina)
⑪ Arturo Prat (Chile)

Ice shelf
Ice cap
Polar pack ice
Drifting ice
Glacier

Scale 1 : 35 000 000

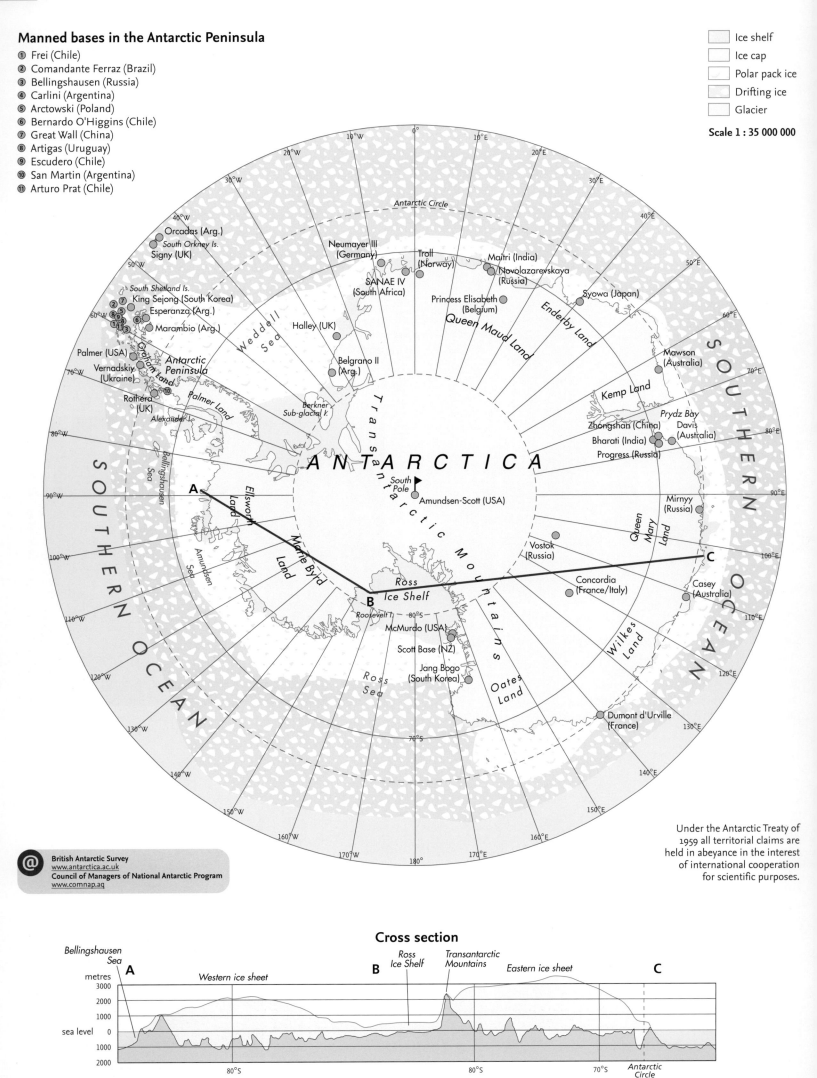

Under the Antarctic Treaty of 1959 all territorial claims are held in abeyance in the interest of international cooperation for scientific purposes.

British Antarctic Survey
www.antarctica.ac.uk
Council of Managers of National Antarctic Program
www.comnap.aq

Cross section

Polar Stereographic projection

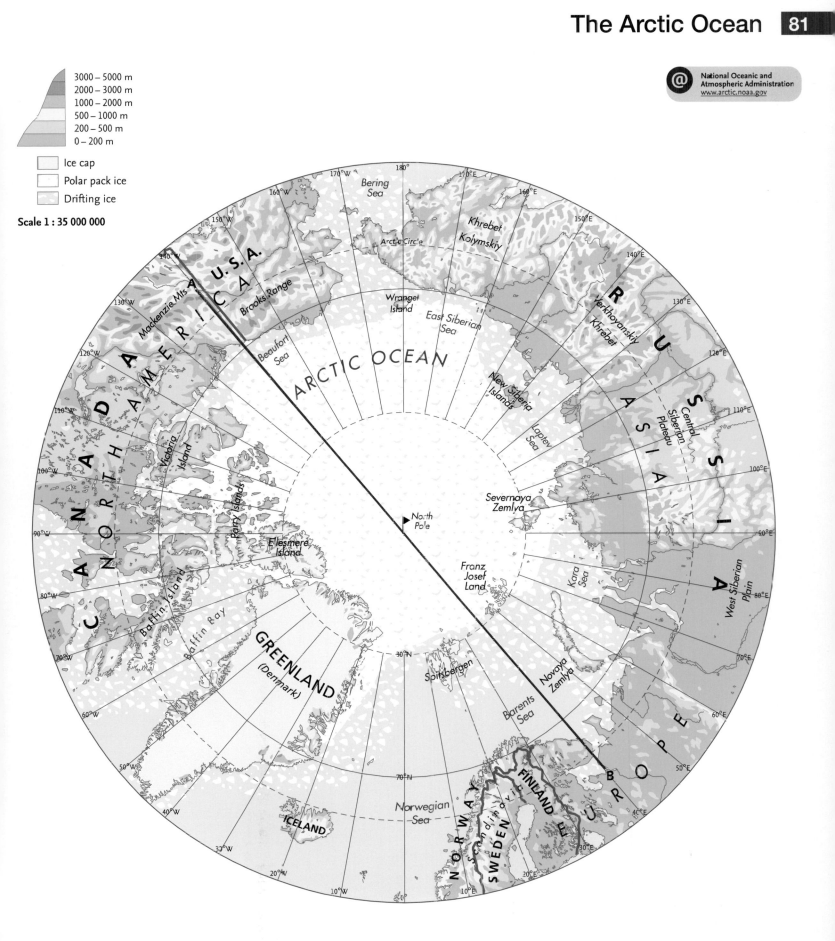

3000 – 5000 m
2000 – 3000 m
1000 – 2000 m
500 – 1000 m
200 – 500 m
0 – 200 m

Ice cap
Polar pack ice
Drifting ice

Scale 1 : 35 000 000

National Oceanic and
Atmospheric Administration
www.arctic.noaa.gov

Bering
Sea

Khrebet
Kolymskiy

Arctic Circle

Wrangel
Island

East Siberian
Sea

Brooks Range

Verkhoyanskiy
Khrebet

Mackenzie Mts

Beaufort
Sea

ARCTIC OCEAN

U.S.A.

NORTH AMERICA

CANADA

New Siberia
Islands

Central
Siberian
Plateau

RUSSIA

ASIA

Laptev
Sea

Victoria
Island

Severnaya
Zemlya

North
Pole

Parry Islands

Ellesmere
Island

Franz
Josef
Land

Kara
Sea

West Siberian
Plain

Baffin Island

Baffin Bay

GREENLAND
(Denmark)

Spitsbergen

Novaya
Zemlya

Barents
Sea

NORWAY

SWEDEN

FINLAND

Scandinavia

EUROPE

Norwegian
Sea

ICELAND

Cross section

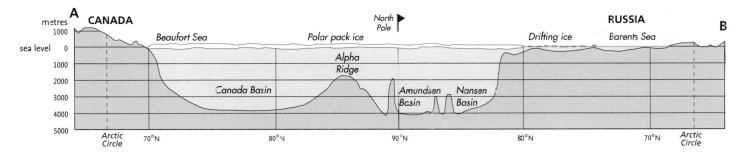

metres   A   CANADA   North
1000   Pole   RUSSIA   B
sea level   Beaufort Sea   Polar pack ice   Drifting ice   Barents Sea
0
                                                    Alpha
1000   Ridge
2000   Canada Basin
3000   Amundsen   Nansen
                                              Basin   Basin
4000
5000   Arctic   70°N   80°N   90°N   80°N   70°N   Arctic
           Circle   Circle

Polar Stereographic projection

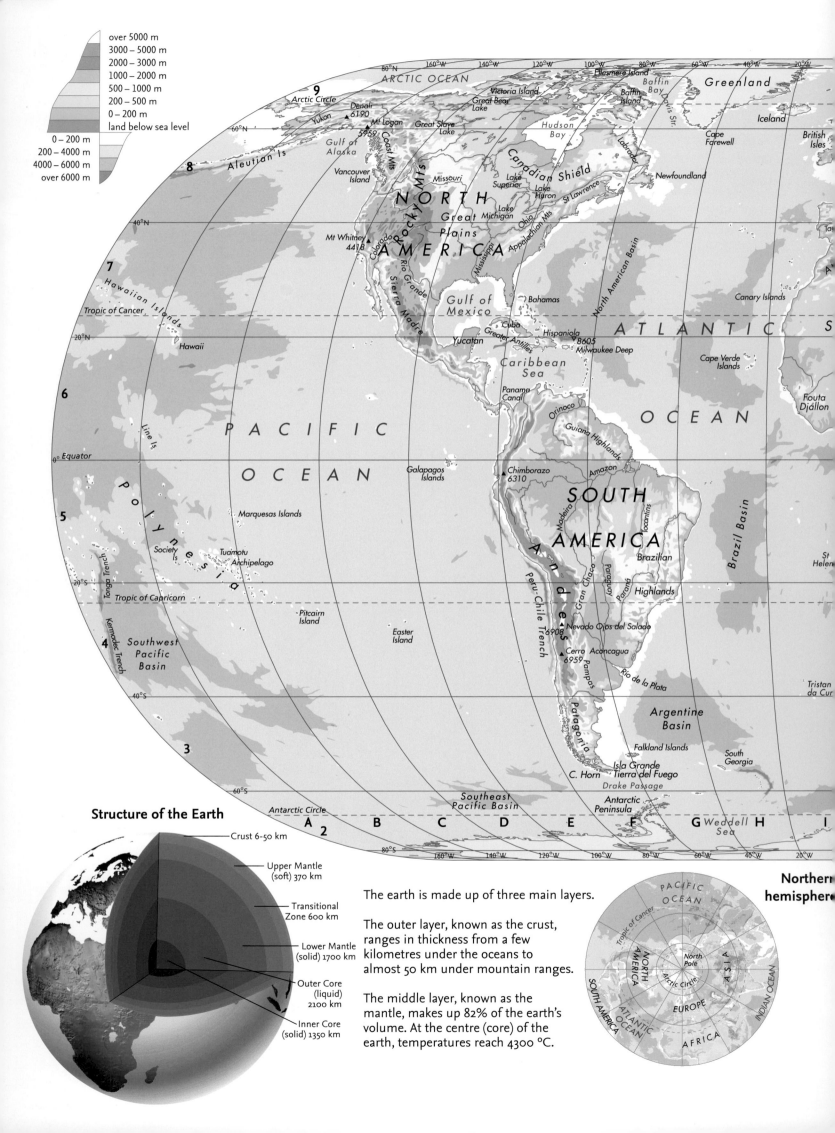

over 5000 m
3000 – 5000 m
2000 – 3000 m
1000 – 2000 m
500 – 1000 m
200 – 500 m
0 – 200 m
land below sea level

0 – 200 m
200 – 4000 m
4000 – 6000 m
over 6000 m

Structure of the Earth

Crust 6-50 km

Upper Mantle
(soft) 370 km

Transitional
Zone 600 km

Lower Mantle
(solid) 1700 km

Outer Core
(liquid)
2100 km

Inner Core
(solid) 1350 km

The earth is made up of three main layers.

The outer layer, known as the crust, ranges in thickness from a few kilometres under the oceans to almost 50 km under mountain ranges.

The middle layer, known as the mantle, makes up 82% of the earth's volume. At the centre (core) of the earth, temperatures reach 4300 °C.

Northern hemisphere

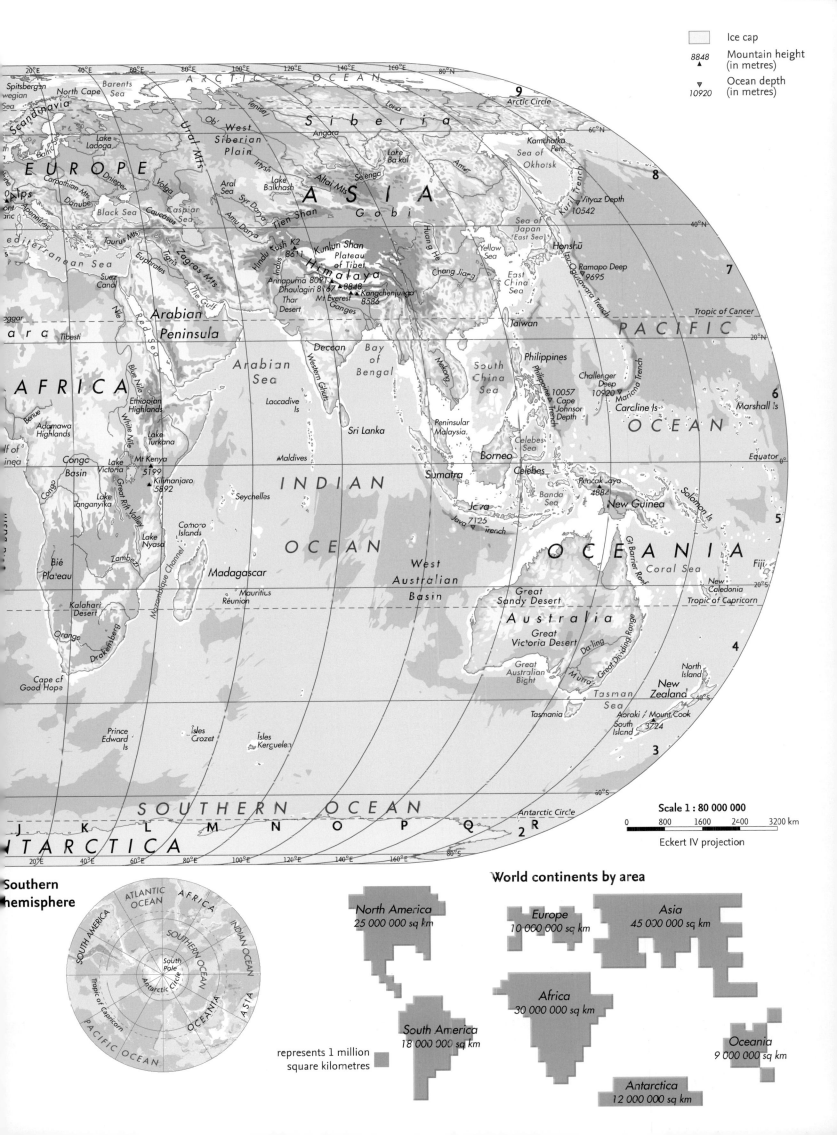

Ice cap

8848 ▲ Mountain height (in metres)

10920 ▼ Ocean depth (in metres)

ARCTIC OCEAN

Spitsbergen
wegian Sea
North Cape
Scandinavia
Barents Sea
20°E 40°E 60°E 80°E 100°E 120°E 140°E 160°E 80°N
9
Siberia
60°N
Lena
Arctic Circle
EUROPE
Baltic
Lake Ladoga
Ural Mts
Ob'
West Siberian Plain
Irtysh
Yenisey
Angara
Lake Baikal
8
Alps
Mont Blanc
Carpathian Mts
Dnieper
Danube
Volga
Black Sea
Caucasus
Caspian Sea
Aral Sea
Syr Darya
Amu Darya
Lake Balkhash
Tien Shan
Altai Mts
ASIA
Gobi
Selenga
Amur
Kamchatka Pen.
Sea of Okhotsk
Kuril Trench
Vityaz Depth 10542
40°N
Mediterranean Sea
Taurus Mts
Zagros Mts
Euphrates
Tigris
Hindu Kush
K2 8611
Indus
Kunlun Shan
Plateau of Tibet
Himalaya
Annapurna 8091 ▲ 8848
Dhaulagiri 8167 ▲ Mt Everest
Thar Desert
Ganges
▲ Kangchenjunga 8586
Huang He
Chang Jiang
Yellow Sea
Sea of Japan (East Sea)
Honshū
Izu-Ogasawara Trench
Ramapo Deep 9695
7
Suez Canal
Nile
Red Sea
Arabian Peninsula
The Gulf
Decean
Western Ghats
Bay of Bengal
Mekong
Taiwan
East China Sea
Tropic of Cancer
20°N
aggar
ara
Tibesti
AFRICA
Benue
Adamawa Highlands
Blue Nile
White Nile
Ethiopian Highlands
Lake Turkana
Arabian Sea
Laccadive Is
Sri Lanka
Maldives
Peninsular Malaysia
South China Sea
Philippines
Philippine Trench
Cape Johnson Depth 10057
Challenger Deep 10920 ▼
Mariana Trench
Caroline Is
PACIFIC
OCEAN
Marshall Is
6
If of inea
Congo Basin
Lake Victoria
Mt Kenya 5199
Kilimanjaro 5892
Great Rift Valley
Lake Tanganyika
Lake Nyasa
Seychelles
INDIAN
OCEAN
Sumatra
Borneo
Celebes
Celebes Sea
Banda Sea
Puncak Jaya 4884
New Guinea
Solomon Is
Equator 0°
5
Congo
Bié Plateau
Zambezi
Comoro Islands
Mozambique Channel
Madagascar
Mauritius
Réunion
Java
Java Trench 7125 ▼
West Australian Basin
OCEANIA
Gt Barrier Reef
Coral Sea
Fiji
New Caledonia
20°S
Kalahari Desert
Orange
Drakensberg
Cape of Good Hope
Isles Crozet
Isles Kerguelen
West Australian Basin
Great Sandy Desert
Australia
Great Victoria Desert
Da Ling
Great Dividing Range
Murray
Great Australian Bight
Tasman Sea
North Island
New Zealand
Aoraki / Mount Cook 3724
South Island
Tropic of Capricorn
4
Prince Edward Is
Tasmania
3
SOUTHERN OCEAN
Antarctic Circle
J K L M N O P Q 2 R
NTARCTICA
20°E 40°E 60°E 80°E 100°E 120°E 140°E 160°E 80°S
40°S
60°S

Scale 1 : 80 000 000

0   800   1600   2400   3200 km

Eckert IV projection

Southern hemisphere

ATLANTIC OCEAN
AFRICA
SOUTH AMERICA
INDIAN OCEAN
SOUTHERN OCEAN
South Pole
Tropic of Capricorn
Antarctic Circle
ASIA
OCEANIA
PACIFIC OCEAN

World continents by area

North America
25 000 000 sq km

Europe
10 000 000 sq km

Asia
45 000 000 sq km

Africa
30 000 000 sq km

South America
18 000 000 sq km

represents 1 million square kilometres

Oceania
9 000 000 sq km

Antarctica
12 000 000 sq km

■ Capital city
○ Other town/city

Abbreviations of country names

SOUTH AMERICA	EUROPE	MA. MACEDONIA
FR.G. FRENCH GUIANA	A. ANDORRA	MO. MOLDOVA
GUY. GUYANA	ALB. ALBANIA	NETH. NETHERLANDS
SUR. SURINAME	AUS. AUSTRIA	RU. RUSSIA
	BEL. BELGIUM	S. SLOVENIA
AFRICA	BELA. BELARUS	SER. SERBIA
B. BURUNDI	B.H. BOSNIA & HERZEGOVINA	SL. SLOVAKIA
BE. BENIN	CR. CROATIA	SW. SWITZERLAND
BUR. BURKINA FASO	CZ. CZECHIA	
CAM. CAMEROON	DEN. DENMARK	ASIA
C.D'I. CÔTE D'IVOIRE	EST. ESTONIA	AR. ARMENIA
EQ. G. EQUATORIAL	GER. GERMANY	AZ. AZERBAIJAN
GUINEA	H. HUNGARY	CYP. CYPRUS
GH. GHANA	K. KOSOVO	GEO. GEORGIA
R. RWANDA	LAT. LATVIA	IS. ISRAEL
T. TOGO	LITH. LITHUANIA	JOR. JORDAN
	LUX. LUXEMBOURG	LEB. LEBANON
	M. MONTENEGRO	U.A.E. UNITED ARAB EMIRATES

International boundaries in the sea shown on this map indicate ownership of islands and island groups only. They do not infer the alignments of legal maritime boundaries.

Time comparisons

Time varies around the world due to the earth's rotation causing different parts of the world to be in light or darkness at any one time. To account for this, the world is divided into twenty-four Standard Time Zones based on 15° intervals of longitude.

1:00am	2:00am	3:00am	4:00am	5:00am	6:00am	7:00am	8:00am	9:00am	10:00am	11:00am	noon
Samoa Tonga (next day)	Hawaiian Is Cook Is Tahiti	Anchorage	Vancouver Seattle Los Angeles	Edmonton Phoenix	Winnipeg Chicago Mexico City	New York Miami Lima	Puerto Rico La Paz Asunción	Nuuk Brasília Buenos Aires	South Georgia	Azores Cape Verde	Reykjavík London Freetown

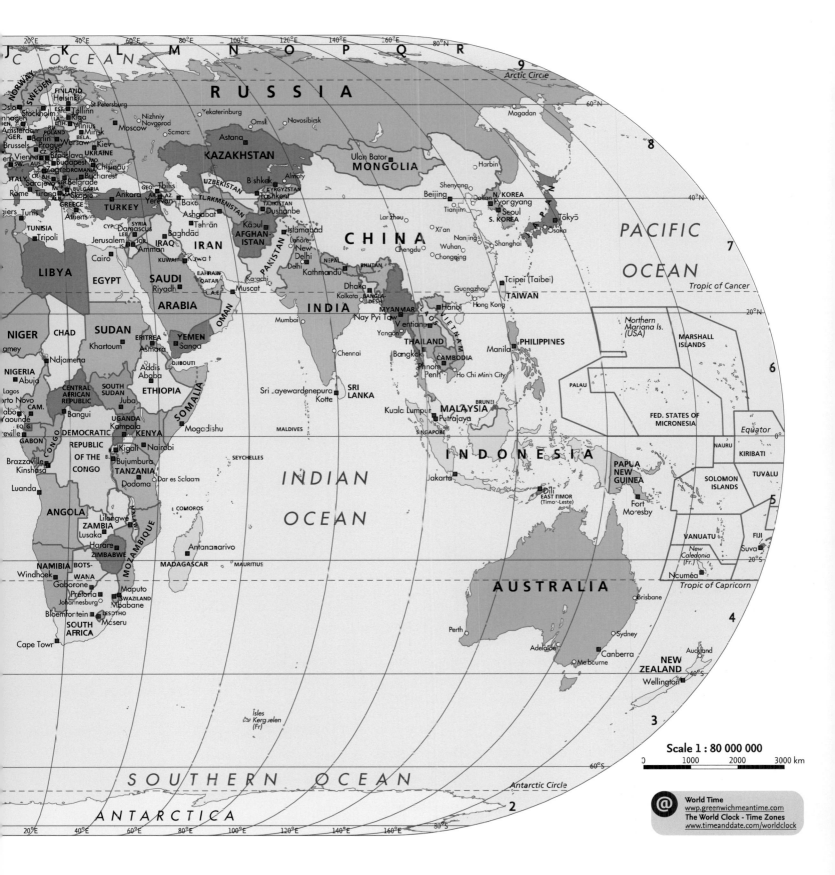

The table below gives examples of times observed at different parts of the world when it is 12 noon in the zone at the Greenwich Meridian (0° longitude). The time at 0° is known as Greenwich Mean Time (GMT).

1:00pm	2:00pm	3:00pm	4:00pm	5:00pm	6:00pm	7:00pm	8:00pm	9:00pm	10:00pm	11:00pm	midnight
Oslo Paris Kinshasa	Helsinki Cairo Cape Town	Moscow Riyadh Dodoma	U.A.E. Mauritius	Yekaterinburg Dushanbe Karachi	Novosibirsk Almaty Dhaka	Bangkok Jakarta	Ulan Bator Hong Kong Perth	Seoul Tōkyō Palau	Port Moresby Brisbane Canberra	Solomon Is Vanuatu New Caledonia	Marshall Is Fiji Wellington

Eckert IV projection

Earthquakes and volcanoes

- ● Earthquake
- ▲ Volcano
- — Plate boundary
- ←→ Direction of movement

Storms and floods

- ⬅ Typical storm path
- ⤻ Rivers that experience major flooding
- ▬ Country affected annually by severe flooding
- 💧 Severe floods causing over 1000 deaths in 1 year (1985–2015)
- 💧 Severe floods causing 500–1000 deaths in 1 year (1985–2015)

Plates

The earth's crust is broken into huge plates which fit together like parts of a giant jigsaw. These float on the semi-molten rock below. The boundaries of the plates are marked by lines of volcanoes and earthquake activity.

Diverging plates

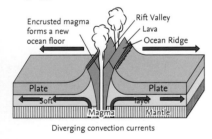

Diverging convection currents

Converging plates

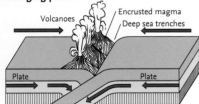

Converging convection currents

Shearing plates

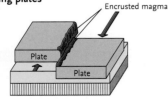

Currents moving past each other

Plate structure: Asia to South America

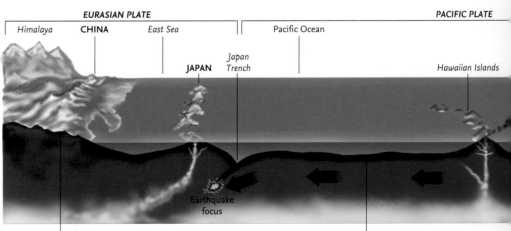

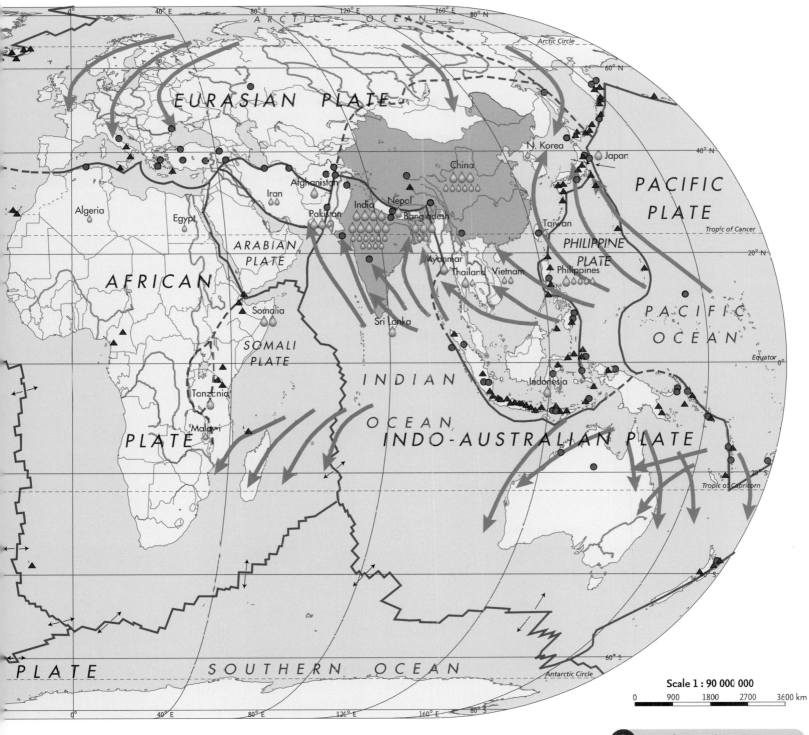

ARCTIC OCEAN

EURASIAN PLATE

PACIFIC PLATE

AFRICAN

ARABIAN PLATE

PACIFIC OCEAN

SOMALI PLATE

PHILIPPINE PLATE

PLATE

INDIAN

OCEAN

INDO-AUSTRALIAN PLATE

SOUTHERN OCEAN

Algeria
Egypt
Iran
Afghanistan
Pakistan
India
Nepal
Bangladesh
Myanmar
Thailand
Vietnam
Philippines
Sri Lanka
Somalia
Tanzania
Malawi
Indonesia
China
N. Korea
Japan
Taiwan

Arctic Circle
Tropic of Cancer
Equator
Tropic of Capricorn
Antarctic Circle

Scale 1 : 90 000 000

0   900   1800   2700   3600 km

USGS Volcano Hazards Program
volcanoes.usgs.gov
USGS National Earthquake Information Center
earthquake.usgs.gov
British Geological Survey
www.bgs.ac.uk

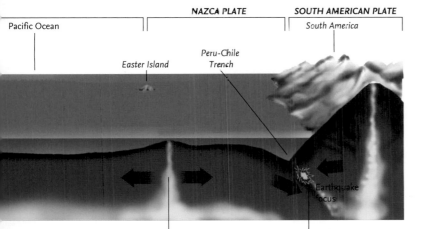

PACIFIC OCEAN
NAZCA PLATE
SOUTH AMERICAN PLATE
South America
Peru-Chile Trench
Easter Island
Earthquake focus
Divergent plates
Convergent plates

Earthquakes

Earthquakes occur most frequently along the junction of plates which make up the earth's crust.
They are caused by the release of stress which builds up at the plate edges. When shock waves from these movements reach the surface they are felt as earthquakes which may result in severe damage to property or loss of lives.

Volcanoes

The greatest number of volcanoes are located in the Pacific 'Ring of Fire'. Violent eruptions often occur when two plates collide and the heat generated forces molten rock (magma) upwards through weaknesses in the earth's crust.

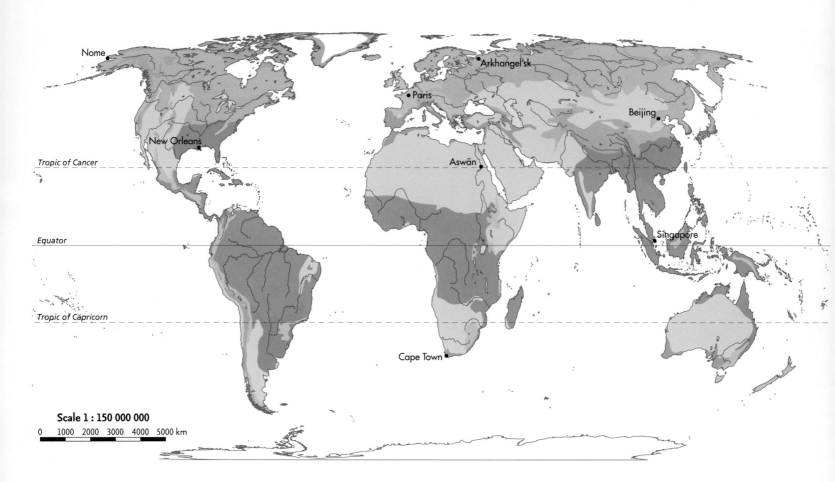

Scale 1 : 150 000 000

0   1000   2000   3000   4000   5000 km

Climate types

☐ **Ice cap**
(very cold and dry)

■ **Tundra and mountain**
(very cold winters, altitude affects climate)

■ **Subarctic**
(rainy climate, with long cold winters)

■ **Continental**
(rainy climate, cold winters, mild / warm summers)

■ **Temperate**
(rainy climate, mild winters, warm summers)

■ **Mediterranean**
(rainy mild winters, dry hot summers)

■ **Subtropical**
(wet warm winters, hot summers)

■ **Tropical**
(constantly hot and wet)

■ **Dry / Arid and Desert**
(dry all year)

• Climate station

@ **World Meteorological Organization**
www.wmo.ch
Met Office World Weather
www.metoffice.gov.uk/weather/world/

Climate graphs

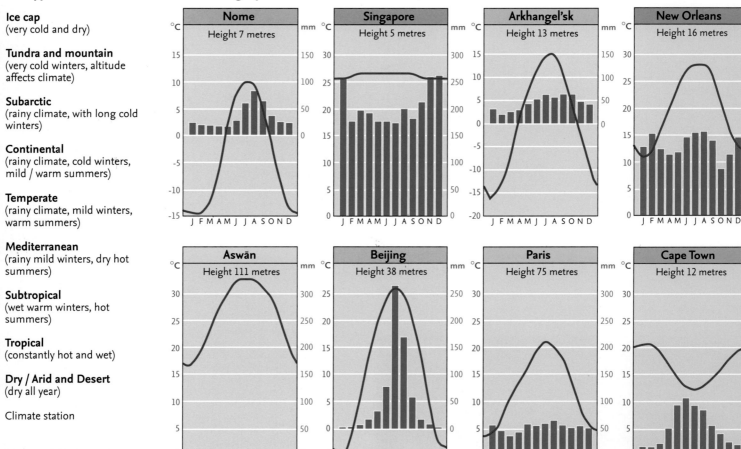

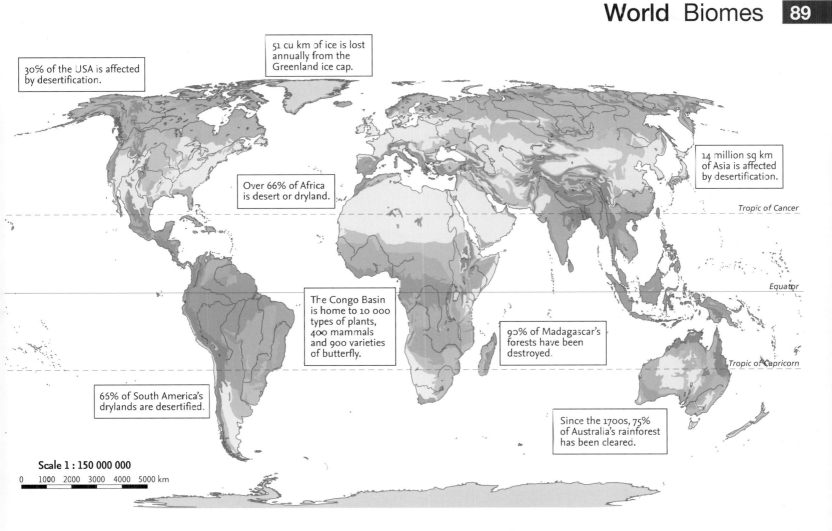

30% of the USA is affected by desertification.

51 cu km of ice is lost annually from the Greenland ice cap.

14 million sq km of Asia is affected by desertification.

Over 66% of Africa is desert or dryland.

Tropic of Cancer

Equator

The Congo Basin is home to 10 000 types of plants, 400 mammals and 900 varieties of butterfly.

90% of Madagascar's forests have been destroyed.

Tropic of Capricorn

66% of South America's drylands are desertified.

Since the 1700s, 75% of Australia's rainforest has been cleared.

Scale 1 : 150 000 000

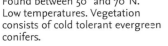

0   1000   2000   3000   4000   5000 km

Types of vegetation

 Ice cap and ice shelf
Extremely cold. No vegetation.

Arctic tundra
Very cold climate. Simple vegetation such as mosses, lichens, grasses and flowering herbs.

Mountain/Alpine
Very low night-time temperatures. Only a few dwarf trees and small leafed shrubs can grow.

Mediterranean
Mild winters and dry summers. Vegetation is mixed shrubs and herbaceous plants.

Savanna grassland
Warm or hot climate. Tropical grasslands with scattered thorn bushes or trees.

Temperate grassland
Grassland is the main vegetation. Summers are hot and winters cold.

Desert
Hot with little rainfall. Very sparse vegetation except cacti and grasses adapted to the harsh conditions.

Boreal/Taiga forest
Found between 50° and 70°N. Low temperatures. Vegetation consists of cold tolerant evergreen conifers.

Coniferous forest
Dense forests of pine, spruce and larch.

Temperate grassland
Grassland is the main vegetation. Summers are hot and winters cold.

Tropical forest
Dense rainforest found in areas of high rainfall near the equator.

Dry tropical forest
Semi deciduous trees with low shrubs and bushes.

Sub tropical forest
Rainfall is seasonal. Vegetation is mainly hard leaf evergreen forest.

Monsoon forest
Areas which experience Monsoon rain. All trees are deciduous.

Rainforests which once grew on 14% of the land surface now cover 6%. Rainforests could disappear completely within 100 years if the current rate of deforestation continues.
Animal habitats are shrinking due to pollution, logging, harmful development and global warming.

World ecosystems

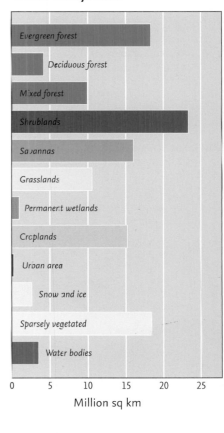

Evergreen forest
Deciduous forest
Mixed forest
Shrublands
Savannas
Grasslands
Permanent wetlands
Croplands
Urban area
Snow and ice
Sparsely vegetated
Water bodies

0   5   10   15   20   25

Million sq km

 **United Nations Environment Programme**
www.unep.org
World Conservation Monitoring Centre
www.unep-wcmc.org
World Resources Institute Earthtrends
earthtrends.wri.org

Eckert IV projection

Global warming

The average temperature of the earth is rising, a process called global warming. Global warming is believed to cause changes to the world's climate which could have serious effects on the environment and people's lives.

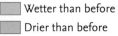 Farmland

Wetter than before

Drier than before

Evidence of global warming

☼ Heat waves

🐚 Ocean warming

Glaciers melting

⬆C Polar temperature rise

Signs of global warming

Spreading diseases

Earlier spring

Plant and animal habitat shifts

Coral damage

Heavy rainfall, snowfall and flooding

Drought and fires

Global temperature difference 1950-2080

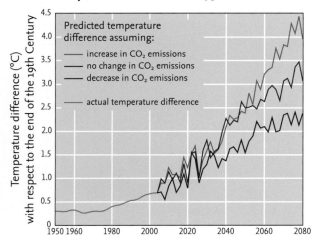

Predicted temperature difference assuming:

— increase in CO₂ emissions
— no change in CO₂ emissions
— decrease in CO₂ emissions

— actual temperature difference

The Greenhouse Effect

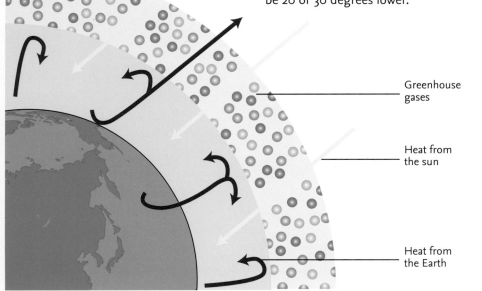

Greenhouse gases build up in the Earth's atmosphere, stopping heat bouncing back into space from the Earth's surface. Without these gases temperatures on Earth would be 20 or 30 degrees lower.

Greenhouse gases

Heat from the sun

Heat from the Earth

Better farming conditions

Shrinking glaciers

Change in ocean currents

More powerful hurricanes

Worse farming conditions

Tropic of Cancer

Equator

Tropic of Capricorn

Fossil fuels are the primary source of carbon dioxide emissions which, along with the other greenhouse gases, are believed to be the principal cause of global climate change.

Evidence of climate change

- Warming oceans
- Shrinking ice sheets
- Declining Arctic sea ice
- Global surface temperature rise
- Sea level rise
- Retreating glaciers
- Ocean acidification
- Extreme events

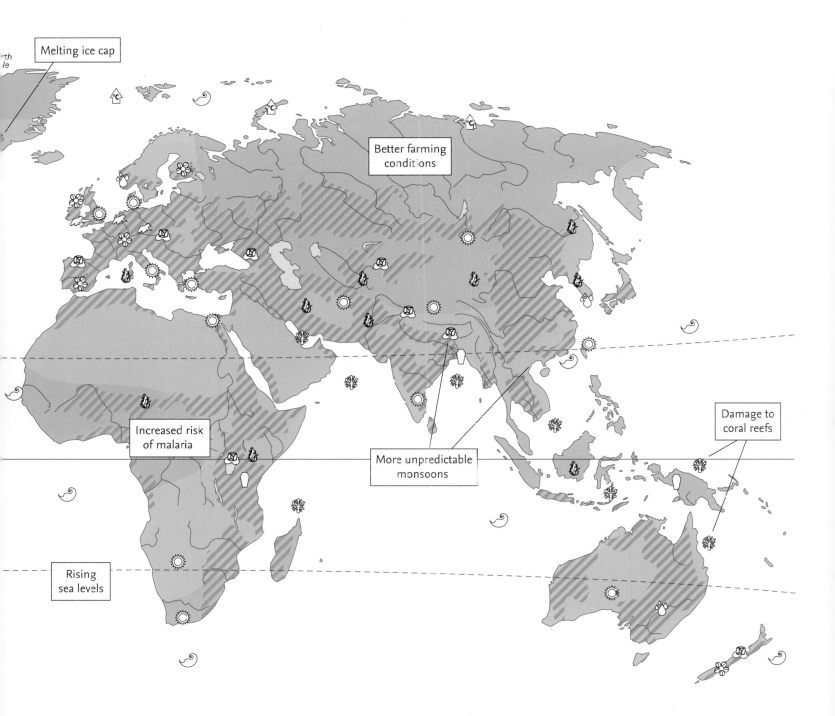

Melting ice cap

Better farming conditions

Increased risk of malaria

More unpredictable monsoons

Damage to coral reefs

Rising sea levels

Projected temperature change

These maps show projected change in annual mean surface air temperature given moderate growth in CO₂ emissions, for three time periods, compared with the average temperature for 1980-1999.

0   1   2   3   4   5   6   7   8°C

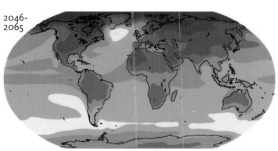

2046-2065

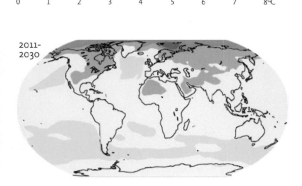

2011-2030

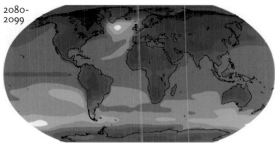

2080-2099

Future trends

- Reduced snow cover and increased thaw

- Decrease in sea ice

- More frequent hot extremes, heat waves and heavy precipitation

- Increased tropical cyclone intensity

- Increase in rainfall in high altitudes

- Decrease in rainfall in sub tropical land regions

- Decrease in water resources in semi-arid areas

World Meteorological Organization
www.wmo.int
Met Office World Weather
www.metoffice.gov.uk/weather/world/
Intergovernmental Panel on Climate Change
www.ipcc.ch

Desertification

- Existing deserts
- Areas at risk of desertification

Deforestation

- Existing tropical forests
- Forests destroyed since 1940

Bushfires

- Recent major forest fires

Water pollution

- Coastal pollution
- River pollution
- Major city with air pollution

Deforestation

Impacts of deforestation

- Flood water carries away unprotected soil

- Without vegetation to soak up water, heavy rain causes floods

- Without humus from rotting leaves, the soil becomes poorer

- Rivers silt up, causing floods and clogging dams

- Burning trees release CO_2 into the atmosphere, adding to 'greenhouse' gases

- Fierce sunshine dries out the earth, making it useless for crops

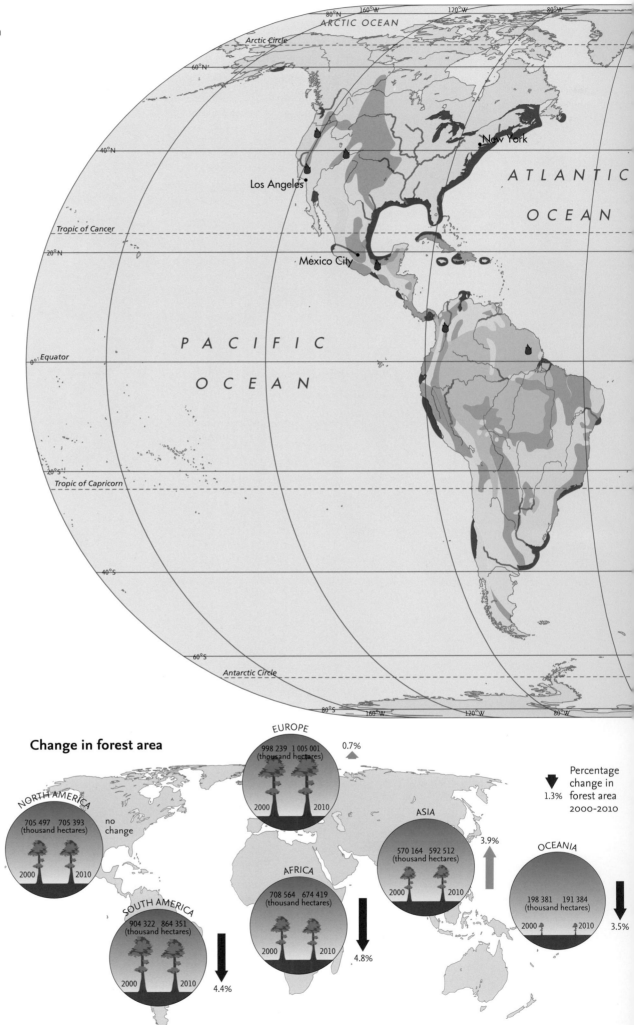

Causes of tropical deforestation 2000-2005

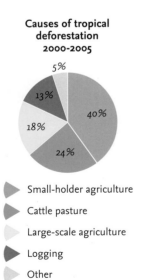

5%
13%
40%
18%
24%

- Small-holder agriculture
- Cattle pasture
- Large-scale agriculture
- Logging
- Other

Change in forest area

EUROPE
998 239   1 005 001
(thousand hectares)
2000   2010
0.7%

NORTH AMERICA
705 497   705 393
(thousand hectares)
2000   2010
no change

ASIA
570 164   592 512
(thousand hectares)
2000   2010
3.9%

AFRICA
708 564   674 419
(thousand hectares)
2000   2010
4.8%

OCEANIA
198 381   191 384
(thousand hectares)
2000   2010
3.5%

SOUTH AMERICA
904 322   864 351
(thousand hectares)
2000   2010
4.4%

Percentage change in forest area 2000-2010
1.3%

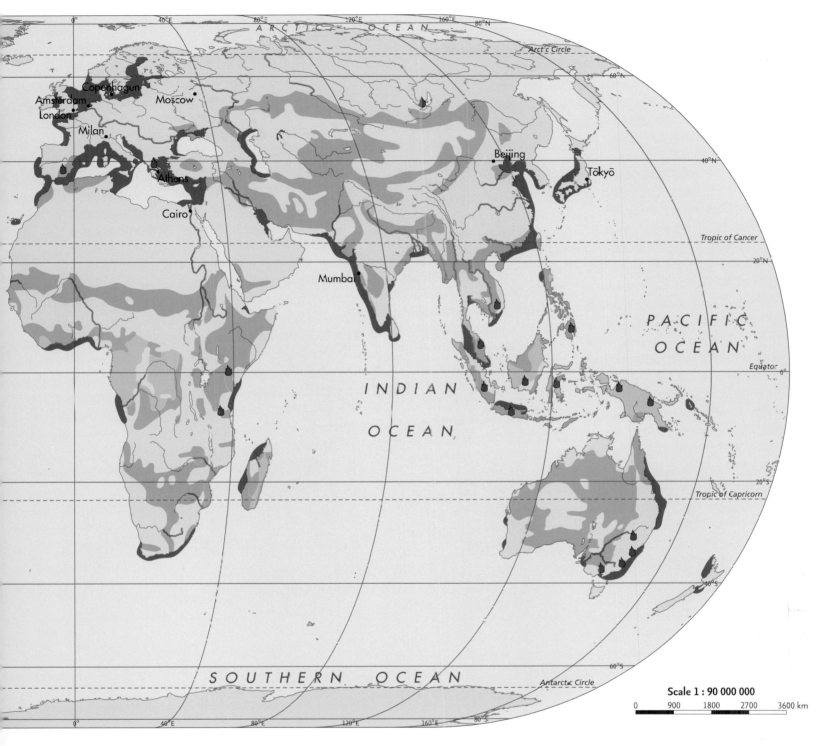

Scale 1 : 90 000 000

0   900   1800   2700   3600 km

Atmospheric pollution: acid rain

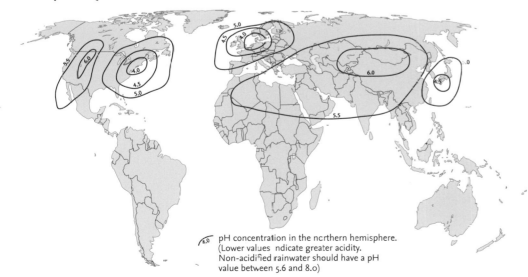

↗6.0 pH concentration in the northern hemisphere.
(Lower values indicate greater acidity.
Non-acidified rainwater should have a pH
value between 5.6 and 8.0)

Impacts of acid rain

- Acidification of water causing widespread damage to plant and animal life

- Essential nutrients are leached from the soil

- Poor health resulting from toxic metals leached from rocks entering the food chain

- Corrosion of buildings

United Nations Environment Programme
www.unep.org
World Conservation Monitoring Centre
www.unep-wcmc.org
World Resources Institute Earthtrends
earthtrends.wri.org
UNESCO World Heritage Sites
whc.unesco.org

Eckert IV projection

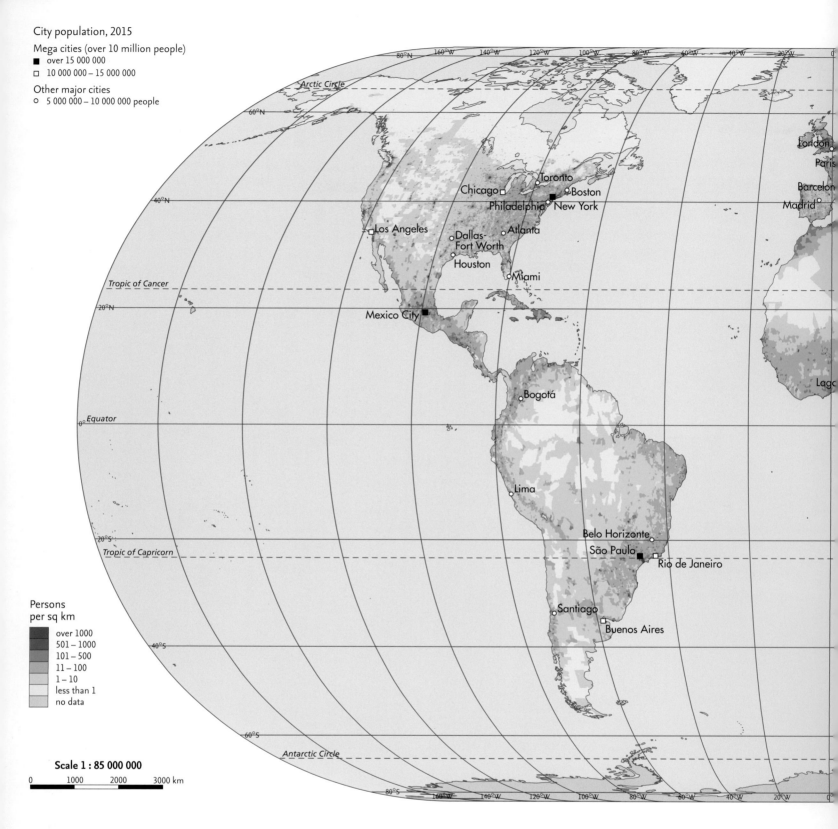

City population, 2015

Mega cities (over 10 million people)
- ■ over 15 000 000
- □ 10 000 000 – 15 000 000

Other major cities
- ○ 5 000 000 – 10 000 000 people

Persons
per sq km

- over 1000
- 501 – 1000
- 101 – 500
- 11 – 100
- 1 – 10
- less than 1
- no data

Scale 1 : 85 000 000

0   1000   2000   3000 km

World population distribution by continents

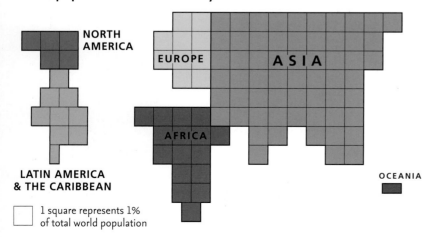

NORTH AMERICA

EUROPE

ASIA

AFRICA

LATIN AMERICA
& THE CARIBBEAN

OCEANIA

☐ 1 square represents 1%
of total world population

Facts about world population

World population, 2015	7 349 472 000
World population, 2050	9 725 148 000
Population 60 years and over, 2015	14.0%
Population 60 years and over, 2050	26.0%
Population under 15 years, 2015	26.1%
Population under 15 years, 2050	21.3%
Life expectancy, 2015-2020	72
Male life expectancy, 2015-2020	69
Female life expectancy, 2015-2020	74

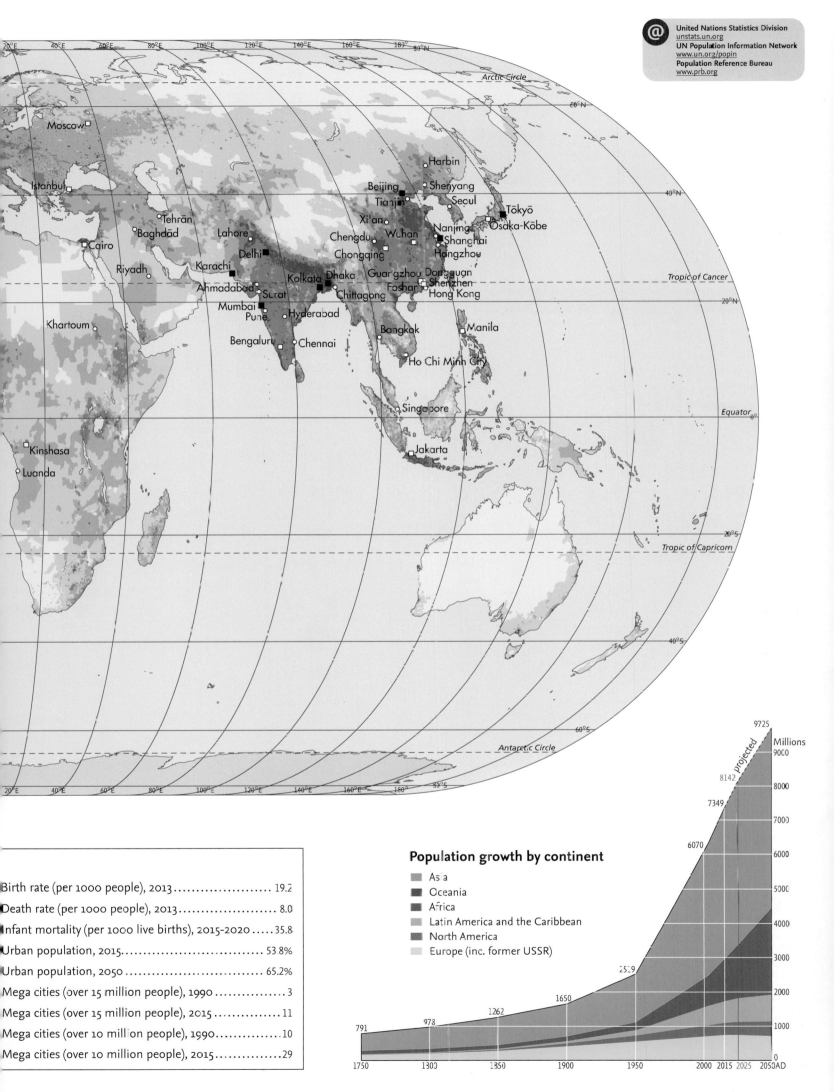

United Nations Statistics Division
unstats.un.org
UN Population Information Network
www.un.org/popin
Population Reference Bureau
www.prb.org

Moscow

Istanbul

Tehrān

Baghdād

Cairo

Riyadh

Khartoum

Kinshasa

Luanda

Lahore

Delhi

Karachi

Ahmadabad

Surat

Mumbai

Pune

Bengaluru

Hyderabad

Chennai

Kolkata

Dhaka

Chittagong

Chengdu

Chongqing

Xi'an

Wuhan

Hangzhou

Guangzhou

Foshan

Dongguan

Shenzhen

Hong Kong

Nanjing

Shanghai

Beijing

Tianjin

Shenyang

Harbin

Seoul

Tōkyō

Osaka-Kōbe

Bangkok

Manila

Ho Chi Minh City

Singapore

Jakarta

Arctic Circle

Tropic of Cancer

Equator

Tropic of Capricorn

Antarctic Circle

Eckert IV projection

Population growth by continent

- Asia
- Oceania
- Africa
- Latin America and the Caribbean
- North America
- Europe (inc. former USSR)

Birth rate (per 1000 people), 2013	19.2
Death rate (per 1000 people), 2013	8.0
Infant mortality (per 1000 live births), 2015–2020	35.8
Urban population, 2015	53.8%
Urban population, 2050	65.2%
Mega cities (over 15 million people), 1990	3
Mega cities (over 15 million people), 2015	11
Mega cities (over 10 million people), 1990	10
Mega cities (over 10 million people), 2015	29

9725

8142

7349

6070

2519

1650

1262

978

791

Millions

projected

9000

8000

7000

6000

5000

4000

3000

2000

1000

0

1750   1800   1850   1900   1950   2000 2015 2025   2050AD

Human Development Index

The Human Development Index is a measure of the well-being of a country. It compares life expectancy, GNI, literacy and the number of years schooling available to each country throughout the world.

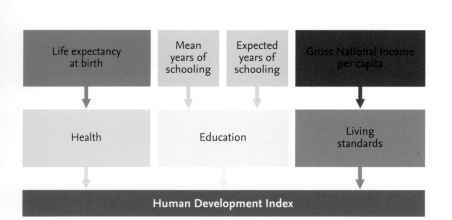

Life expectancy at birth	Mean years of schooling	Expected years of schooling	Gross National Income per capita
Health	Education		Living standards

Human Development Index

Norway
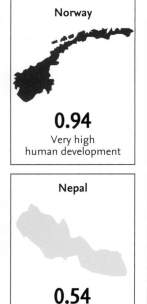
0.94
Very high
human development

Russia
0.78
High
human development

Indonesia
0.68
Medium
human development

Mozambique
0.39
Low
human development

Nepal
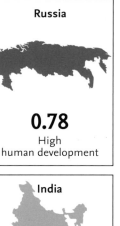
0.54
Low
human development

India

0.59
Medium
human development

Ecuador
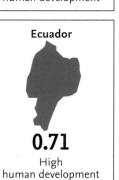
0.71
High
human development

United Kingdom
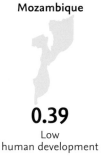
0.89
Very high
human development

Life expectancy

Life expectancy is the average age a newborn infant would live to if patterns of mortality prevailing for all people at the time of its birth were to stay the same throughout its life.

Life expectancy in years

	80 – 83
	71 – 79.9
	60 – 70.9 average
	50 – 59.9
	45 – 49.9
	no data

World average 71.
Statistics are for 2012.

Scale 1 : 190 000 000

0   2000   4000   6000   8000 km

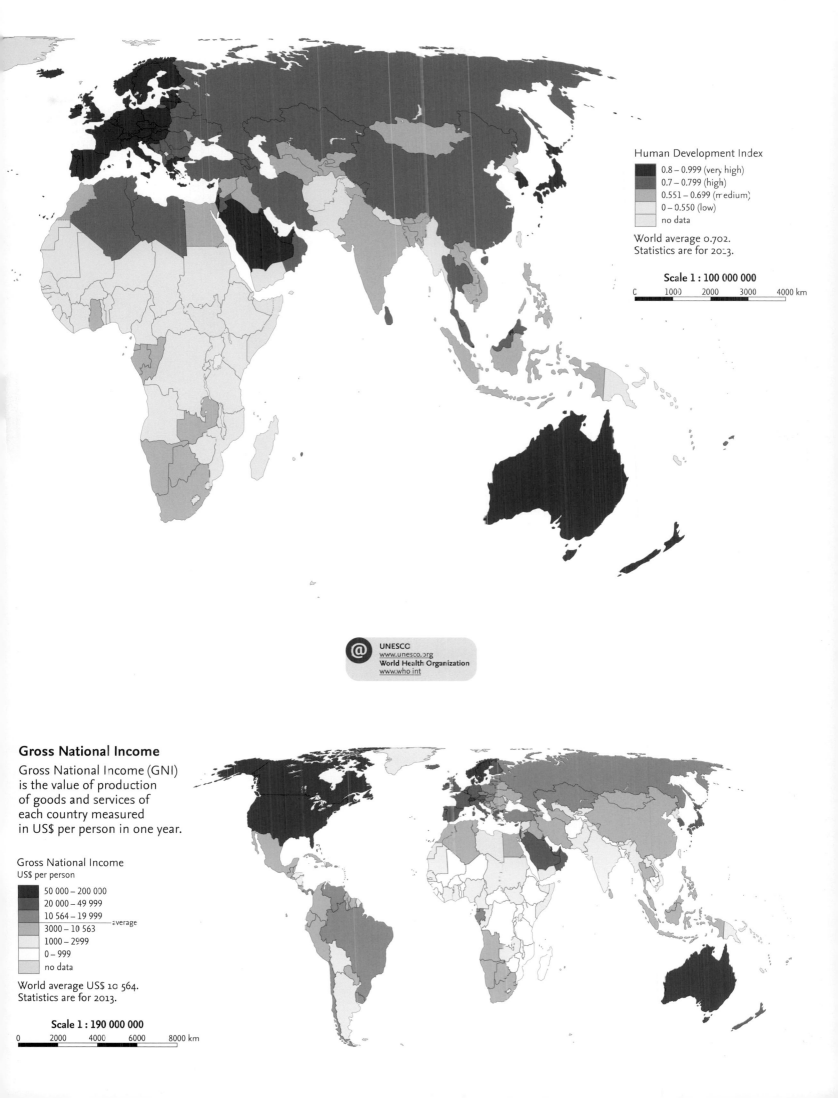

Human Development Index
- 0.8 – 0.999 (very high)
- 0.7 – 0.799 (high)
- 0.551 – 0.699 (medium)
- 0 – 0.550 (low)
- no data

World average 0.702.
Statistics are for 2013.

Scale 1 : 100 000 000

0   1000   2000   3000   4000 km

UNESCO
www.unesco.org
World Health Organization
www.who.int

Gross National Income

Gross National Income (GNI) is the value of production of goods and services of each country measured in US$ per person in one year.

Gross National Income
US$ per person
- 50 000 – 200 000
- 20 000 – 49 999
- 10 564 – 19 999 — average
- 3000 – 10 563
- 1000 – 2999
- 0 – 999
- no data

World average US$ 10 564.
Statistics are for 2013.

Scale 1 : 190 000 000

0   2000   4000   6000   8000 km

Flag	Country	Capital city	Area sq km	Total population 2015	Density persons per sq km 2015	Birth rate per 1000 population 2013	Life expectancy in years 2013	Urban population % 2014	Population change annual % 2014
	Afghanistan	Kābul	652 225	32 527 000	50	34	61	26	2.4
	Albania	Tirana	28 748	2 897 000	101	13	78	56	-0.1
	Algeria	Algiers	2 381 741	39 667 000	17	24	71	70	1.8
	Andorra	Andorra la Vella	465	70 000	151	..	..	86	1.2
	Angola	Luanda	1 246 700	25 022 000	20	44	52	43	3.1
	Antigua & Barbuda	St John's	442	92 000	208	16	76	24	1.0
	Argentina	Buenos Aires	2 766 889	43 417 000	16	17	76	92	0.9
	Armenia	Yerevan	29 800	3 018 000	101	14	75	63	0.2
	Australia	Canberra	7 692 024	23 969 000	3	13	82	89	1.6
	Austria	Vienna	83 855	8 545 000	102	9	81	66	0.6
	Azerbaijan	Baku	86 600	9 754 000	113	18	71	54	1.3
	Bahamas, The	Nassau	13 939	388 000	28	15	75	83	1.4
	Bahrain	Manama	691	1 377 000	1993	15	77	89	0.9
	Bangladesh	Dhaka	143 998	160 996 000	1118	20	71	34	1.2
	Barbados	Bridgetown	430	284 000	660	13	75	32	0.5
	Belarus	Minsk	207 600	9 496 000	46	13	72	76	0.0
	Belgium	Brussels	30 520	11 299 000	370	11	80	98	0.4
	Belize	Belmopan	22 965	359 000	16	23	74	44	2.3
	Benin	Porto-Novo	112 620	10 880 000	97	36	59	44	2.6
	Bhutan	Thimphu	46 620	775 000	17	20	68	38	1.5
	Bolivia	La Paz/Sucre	1 098 581	10 725 000	10	26	67	68	1.6
	Bosnia and Herzegovina	Sarajevo	51 130	3 810 000	75	9	76	40	-0.1
	Botswana	Gaborone	581 370	2 262 000	4	24	47	57	0.9
	Brazil	Brasília	8 514 879	207 848 000	24	15	74	85	0.8
	Brunei	Bandar Seri Begawan	5 765	423 000	73	16	79	77	1.3
	Bulgaria	Sofia	110 994	7 150 000	64	9	74	74	-0.5
	Burkina Faso	Ouagadougou	274 200	18 106 000	66	41	56	29	2.8
	Burundi	Bujumbura	27 835	11 179 000	402	45	54	12	3.1
	Cambodia	Phnom Penh	181 035	15 578 000	86	26	72	21	1.8
	Cameroon	Yaoundé	475 442	23 344 000	49	37	55	54	2.5
	Canada	Ottawa	9 984 670	35 940 000	4	11	81	82	1.1
	Cape Verde	Praia	4 033	521 000	129	20	75	65	0.9
	Central African Republic	Bangui	622 436	4 900 000	8	34	50	40	2.0
	Chad	Ndjamena	1 284 000	14 037 000	11	46	51	22	3.0
	Chile	Santiago	756 945	17 948 000	24	14	80	89	0.9
	China	Beijing	9 606 802	1 383 925 000	144	12	75	54	0.5
	Colombia	Bogotá	1 141 748	48 229 000	42	19	74	76	1.3
	Comoros	Moroni	1 862	788 000	423	35	61	28	2.4
	Congo	Brazzaville	342 000	4 620 000	14	38	59	65	2.5
	Congo, Dem. Rep. of the	Kinshasa	2 345 410	77 267 000	33	43	50	42	2.7
	Costa Rica	San José	51 100	4 808 000	94	15	80	76	1.3
	Côte d'Ivoire	Yamoussoukro	322 463	22 702 000	70	37	51	53	2.4
	Croatia	Zagreb	56 538	4 240 000	75	9	77	59	-0.5
	Cuba	Havana	110 860	11 390 000	103	10	179	77	-0.1
	Cyprus	Nicosia	9 251	1 165 000	126	11	80	67	1.0
	Czechia	Prague	78 864	10 543 000	134	10	78	73	0.0
	Denmark	Copenhagen	43 075	5 669 000	132	10	80	88	0.4
	Djibouti	Djibouti	23 200	888 000	38	27	62	77	1.5

.. no data available

Flag	Country	Capital city	Area sq km	Total population 2015	Density persons per sq km 2015	Birth rate per 1000 population 2013	Life expectancy in years 2013	Urban population % 2014	Population change annual % 2014
	Dominica	Roseau	750	73 000	97	..	..	69	0.5
	Dominican Republic	Santo Domingo	48 442	10 528 000	217	21	73	78	1.2
	East Timor	Dili	14 874	1 185 000	80	36	68	32	2.7
	Ecuador	Quito	272 045	16 144 000	59	21	76	64	1.5
	Egypt	Cairo	1 001 450	91 508 000	91	23	71	43	1.6
	El Salvador	San Salvador	21 041	6 127 000	291	20	72	66	0.7
	Equatorial Guinea	Malabo	28 051	845 000	30	35	53	40	2.7
	Eritrea	Asmara	117 400	5 228 000	45	37	63	22	3.2
	Estonia	Tallinn	45 200	1 313 000	29	10	76	68	-0.3
	Ethiopia	Addis Ababa	1 133 880	99 391 000	88	33	64	19	2.5
	Fiji	Suva	18 330	892 000	49	20	70	53	0.7
	Finland	Helsinki	338 145	5 503 000	16	11	81	84	0.5
	France	Paris	543 965	64 395 000	118	12	82	79	0.4
	Gabon	Libreville	267 667	1 725 000	6	32	63	87	2.3
	Gambia, The	Banjul	11 295	1 991 000	176	43	59	59	3.2
	Georgia	Tbilisi	69 700	4 000 000	57	13	74	53	0.4
	Germany	Berlin	357 022	80 689 000	226	9	81	75	0.3
	Ghana	Accra	238 537	27 410 000	115	31	61	53	2.1
	Greece	Athens	131 957	10 955 000	83	9	81	78	-0.6
	Grenada	St George's	348	107 000	283	19	73	36	0.4
	Guatemala	Guatemala City	108 890	16 343 000	150	31	72	51	2.5
	Guinea	Conakry	245 857	12 609 000	51	37	56	37	2.5
	Guinea-Bissau	Bissau	36 125	1 844 000	51	37	54	49	2.4
	Guyana	Georgetown	214 969	767 000	4	20	66	28	0.5
	Haiti	Port-au-Prince	27 750	10 711 000	386	26	63	57	1.4
	Honduras	Tegucigalpa	112 088	8 075 000	72	26	74	54	2.0
	Hungary	Budapest	93 030	9 855 000	106	9	75	71	-0.3
	Iceland	Reykjavík	102 820	329 000	3	13	83	94	1.2
	India	New Delhi	3 166 620	1 311 051 000	414	20	66	32	1.2
	Indonesia	Jakarta	1 919 445	257 564 000	134	19	71	53	1.2
	Iran	Tehrān	1 648 000	79 109 000	48	19	74	73	1.3
	Iraq	Baghdād	438 317	36 423 000	83	31	69	69	2.5
	Ireland	Dublin	70 282	4 688 000	67	15	81	63	0.3
	Israel	Jerusalem*	22 072	8 064 000	365	21	82	92	1.9
	Italy	Rome	301 245	59 798 000	199	9	82	69	1.8
	Jamaica	Kingston	10 991	2 793 000	254	14	73	55	0.2
	Japan	Tōkyō	377 727	126 573 000	335	8	83	93	-0.2
	Jordan	‘Ammān	89 206	7 595 000	85	27	74	83	2.3
	Kazakhstan	Astana	2 717 300	17 625 000	6	23	70	53	1.5
	Kenya	Nairobi	582 646	46 050 000	79	35	62	25	2.7
	Kiribati	Bairiki	717	112 000	156	23	69	44	1.5
	Kosovo	Priština	10 908	1 805 000	165	18	71	..	0.3
	Kuwait	Kuwait	17 818	3 892 000	218	21	74	98	3.2
	Kyrgyzstan	Bishkek	198 500	5 940 000	30	27	70	36	2.0
	Laos	Vientiane	236 800	6 802 000	29	27	68	38	1.8
	Latvia	Rīga	64 589	1 971 000	31	10	74	67	-1.1
	Lebanon	Beirut	10 452	5 851 000	560	13	80	88	1.0
	Lesotho	Maseru	30 355	2 135 000	70	27	49	27	1.1

Flag	Country	Capital city	Area sq km	Total population 2015	Density persons per sq km 2015	Birth rate per 1000 population 2013	Life expectancy in years 2013	Urban population % 2014	Population change annual % 2014
	Liberia	Monrovia	111 369	4 503 000	40	35	61	49	2.4
	Libya	Tripoli	1 759 540	6 278 000	4	21	75	78	0.8
	Liechtenstein	Vaduz	160	38 000	238	9	82	14	0.7
	Lithuania	Vilnius	65 200	2 878 000	44	10	74	67	-1.0
	Luxembourg	Luxembourg	2 586	567 000	219	11	82	90	2.3
	Macedonia	Skopje	25 713	2 078 000	81	11	75	57	0.1
	Madagascar	Antananarivo	587 041	24 235 000	41	35	65	34	2.8
	Malawi	Lilongwe	118 484	17 215 000	145	40	55	16	2.8
	Malaysia	Kuala Lumpur/Putrajaya	332 965	30 331 000	91	18	75	74	1.6
	Maldives	Male	298	364 000	1221	22	78	44	1.9
	Mali	Bamako	1 240 140	17 600 000	14	47	55	39	3.0
	Malta	Valletta	316	419 000	1326	10	81	95	0.9
	Marshall Islands	Dalap-Uliga-Darrit	181	53 000	293	..	..	72	0.3
	Mauritania	Nouakchott	1 030 700	4 068 000	4	34	62	59	2.4
	Mauritius	Port Louis	2 040	1 273 000	624	11	74	40	0.2
	Mexico	Mexico City	1 972 545	127 017 000	64	18	77	79	1.2
	Micronesia, Fed. States of	Palikir	701	526 000	750	24	69	22	0.3
	Moldova	Chișinău	33 700	4 069 000	121	12	69	45	-0.1
	Mongolia	Ulan Bator	1 565 000	2 959 000	2	23	68	71	1.5
	Montenegro	Podgorica	13 812	626 000	45	12	75	64	0.1
	Morocco	Rabat	446 550	34 378 000	77	23	71	60	1.5
	Mozambique	Maputo	799 380	27 978 000	35	39	50	32	2.4
	Myanmar	Nay Pyi Taw	676 577	53 897 000	80	17	65	34	0.9
	Namibia	Windhoek	824 292	2 459 000	3	26	64	46	1.9
	Nepal	Kathmandu	147 181	28 514 000	194	21	68	18	1.2
	Netherlands	Amsterdam/The Hague	41 526	16 925 000	408	10	81	90	0.3
	New Zealand	Wellington	270 534	4 529 000	17	13	81	86	1.5
	Nicaragua	Managua	130 000	6 082 000	47	23	75	58	1.4
	Niger	Niamey	1 267 000	19 899 000	16	50	58	18	3.9
	Nigeria	Abuja	923 768	182 202 000	197	41	52	47	2.8
	North Korea	Pyongyang	120 538	25 155 000	209	14	70	61	0.5
	Norway	Oslo	323 878	5 211 000	16	12	81	80	1.1
	Oman	Muscat	309 500	4 491 000	15	21	77	77	7.8
	Pakistan	Islamabad	881 888	188 925 000	214	25	67	38	1.6
	Palau	Melekeok	497	21 000	42	13	..	86	0.9
	Panama	Panama City	77 082	3 929 000	51	19	78	66	1.6
	Papua New Guinea	Port Moresby	462 840	7 619 000	16	29	62	13	2.1
	Paraguay	Asunción	406 752	6 639 000	16	24	72	59	1.7
	Peru	Lima	1 285 216	31 377 000	24	20	75	78	1.3
	Philippines	Manila	300 000	100 699 000	336	24	69	44	1.7
	Poland	Warsaw	312 683	38 612 000	123	10	77	61	-0.1
	Portugal	Lisbon	88 940	10 350 000	116	8	80	63	-0.6
	Qatar	Doha	11 437	2 235 000	195	11	79	99	4.5
	Romania	Bucharest	237 500	19 511 000	82	9	74	54	-0.4
	Russia	Moscow	17 075 400	143 457 000	8	13	71	74	0.2
	Rwanda	Kigali	26 338	11 610 000	441	35	64	28	2.7
	St Kitts & Nevis	Basseterre	261	56 000	215	..	..	32	1.1
	St Lucia	Castries	617	185 000	300	15	75	18	0.7

.. no data available

Flag	Country	Capital city	Area sq km	Total population 2015	Density persons per sq km 2015	Birth rate per 1000 population 2013	Life expectancy in years 2013	Urban population % 2014	Population change annual % 2014
	St Vincent & the Grenadines	Kingstown	389	109 000	280	16	73	50	0.0
	Samoa	Apia	2 831	193 000	68	26	73	19	0.8
	San Marino	San Marino	61	32 000	525	..	..	94	0.6
	São Tomé & Príncipe	São Tomé	964	190 000	197	34	66	65	2.5
	Saudi Arabia	Riyadh	2 200 000	31 540 000	14	19	76	83	1.9
	Senegal	Dakar	196 720	15 129 000	77	38	63	43	2.9
	Serbia	Belgrade	77 453	7 046 000	91	9	75	55	-0.5
	Seychelles	Victoria	455	96 000	211	19	74	54	1.8
	Sierra Leone	Freetown	71 740	6 453 000	90	37	46	40	1.8
	Singapore	Singapore	639	5 604 000	8770	9	82	100	1.3
	Slovakia	Bratislava	49 035	5 426 000	111	10	76	54	0.1
	Slovenia	Ljubljana	20 251	2 063 000	102	10	80	50	0.1
	Solomon Islands	Honiara	28 370	584 000	21	31	68	22	2.1
	Somalia	Mogadishu	637 657	10 787 000	17	44	55	39	2.9
	South Africa	Pretoria/Cape Town/Bloemfontein	1 219 090	54 490 000	45	21	57	64	1.6
	South Korea	Seoul	99 274	50 293 000	507	9	81	82	0.4
	South Sudan	Juba	644 329	12 340 000	19	36	55	19	3.8
	Spain	Madrid	504 782	46 122 000	91	9	82	79	-0.5
	Sri Lanka	Sri Jayewardenepura Kotte	65 610	20 715 000	316	18	74	18	0.8
	Sudan	Khartoum	1 861 484	40 235 000	22	33	62	34	2.1
	Suriname	Paramaribo	163 820	543 000	3	18	71	66	0.9
	Swaziland	Mbabane	17 364	1 287 000	74	30	49	21	1.4
	Sweden	Stockholm	449 964	9 779 000	22	12	82	86	0.9
	Switzerland	Bern	41 293	8 299 000	201	10	83	74	1.2
	Syria	Damascus	184 026	18 502 000	101	24	75	57	2.0
	Taiwan	Taipei	36 179	23 462 000	648	..	..	..	..
	Tajikistan	Dushanbe	143 100	8 482 000	59	33	67	27	2.4
	Tanzania	Dodoma	945 087	53 470 000	57	39	61	31	3.0
	Thailand	Bangkok	513 115	67 959 000	132	10	74	49	0.3
	Togo	Lomé	56 785	7 305 000	129	36	56	39	2.6
	Tonga	Nuku'alofa	748	106 000	142	25	73	24	0.4
	Trinidad & Tobago	Port of Spain	5 128	1 360 000	265	14	70	9	0.2
	Tunisia	Tunis	164 150	11 254 000	69	20	74	67	1.0
	Turkey	Ankara	779 452	78 666 000	101	17	75	73	1.2
	Turkmenistan	Ashgabat	488 100	5 374 000	11	21	65	50	1.3
	Uganda	Kampala	241 038	39 032 000	162	43	59	16	3.3
	Ukraine	Kiev	603 700	44 824 000	74	11	71	69	-0.3
	United Arab Emirates	Abu Dhabi	77 700	9 157 000	118	14	77	85	1.1
	United Kingdom	London	243 609	64 716 000	266	12	81	82	0.6
	United States of America	Washington	9 826 635	321 774 000	33	13	79	81	0.7
	Uruguay	Montevideo	176 215	3 432 000	19	14	77	95	0.3
	Uzbekistan	Tashkent	447 400	29 893 000	67	23	68	36	1.6
	Vanuatu	Port Vila	12 190	265 000	22	27	72	26	2.2
	Venezuela	Caracas	912 050	31 108 000	34	20	75	89	1.5
	Vietnam	Hanoi	329 565	93 448 000	284	16	76	33	1.1
	Yemen	Sanaa	527 968	26 832 000	51	31	63	34	2.3
	Zambia	Lusaka	752 614	16 212 000	22	43	58	40	3.3
	Zimbabwe	Harare	390 759	15 603 000	40	31	60	33	3.1

.. no data available

The important names on the reference maps in the atlas are found in the index.
The names are listed in alphabetical order. Each entry gives the country or region of the
world in which the name is located followed by the page number, its alphanumeric grid
reference and then its co-ordinates of latitude and longitude. Names of very large areas
may have these co-ordinates omitted. Area names which are included in the index are
referenced to the centre of the feature. In the case of rivers, the mouth or confluence
is taken as the point of reference. It is therefore necessary to follow the river upstream
from this point to find its name on the map.

On the map of part of Ireland to the right Dublin is found in grid square E3 at latitude
53° 21'N longitude 6° 18'W.

This appears in the index as   Dublin Ireland 25 E3 53.21N 6.18W .
The chart below explains all the elements listed for each entry.

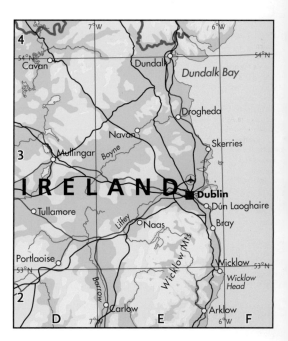

Dublin	Ireland	25	E3	53.21N	6.18W
Name of the feature to be located.	Name of the country in which the feature is situated.	Page in the atlas where the feature is shown on the largest scale.	Grid square where the feature is found.	Degrees and minutes north or south of the equator.	Degrees and minutes east or west of Greenwich meridian.

Sometimes an abbreviated description of a feature is included in the entry.
A list of abbreviations used in the index is included below.

Abbreviations

Afghan.	Afghanistan	Dem. Rep.	Democratic Republic of	Mt.	Mount	resr.	reservoir
Austa.	Australasia	Congo	the Congo	mtn.	mountain	Serb.	Serbia
b., **B.**	bay, Bay	Equat. Guinea	Equatorial Guinea	mts., **Mts.**	mountains	S. Africa	South Africa
Bangla.	Bangladesh	est.	estuary	N. America	North America	S. America	South America
Bosnia.	Bosnia and Herzegovina	f.	physical feature eg. valley,	Neth.	Netherlands	S. Korea	South Korea
c., **C.**	cape, Cape		plain	N. Korea	North Korea	str., **Str.**	strait, Strait
C. America	Central America	**G.**	Gulf	**Oc.**	Ocean	Switz.	Switzerland
C.A.R.	Central African Republic	I.o.M	Isle of Man	pen., **Pen.**	peninsula, Peninsula	U.K.	United Kingdom
d.	Internal division eg. state,	l. **L.**	lake, Lake	Phil.	Philippines	U.S.A.	United States of America
	county	Lux.	Luxembourg	P.N.G.	Papua New Guinea	W. Sahara	Western Sahara
des.	desert	Mont.	Montenegro	r.	river		

A

Aberdeen Scotland **24 F4** 57.08N 2.07W
Aberystwyth Wales **23 C4** 52.25N 4.06W
Abidjan Côte d'Ivoire **56 C5** 5.19N 4.01W
Abu Dhabi U.A.E. **42 E3** 24.27N 54.23E
Abuja Nigeria **56 D5** 9.12N 7.11E
Acapulco Mexico **65 J4** 16.51N 99.56W
Accra Ghana **56 C5** 5.33N 0.15W
Aconcagua, Cerro mtn. Argentina **69 D3**
  32.37S 70.00W
Adamawa Highlands Nigeria/Cameroon **56 E5**
  7.05N 12.00E
Adana Turkey **31 G2** 37.00N 35.19E
Addis Ababa Ethiopia **56 G5** 9.03N 38.42E
Adelaide Australia **76 D2** 34.56S 138.36E
Aden, G. of Indian Oc. **42 D2** 13.00N 50.00E
Adriatic Sea Med. Sea **32 F5** 42.30N 16.00E
Aegean Sea Med. Sea **30 F2** 39.00N 25.00E
Afghanistan Asia **42 F4** 33.00N 65.30E
Africa 54–57
Ahmadabad India **43 G3** 23.03N 72.40E
Albania Europe **30 E3** 41.00N 20.00E
Aleppo Syria **42 C4** 36.14N 37.10E
Alexandria Egypt **56 F8** 31.13N 29.55E
Algeria Africa **56 C7** 28.00N 2.00E
Algiers Algeria **56 D8** 36.50N 3.00E
Alice Springs Australia **76 D3** 23.42S 133.52E
Allier r. France **30 D3** 46.58N 3.04E
Alps mts. Europe **30 D3** 46.00N 7.30E
Altai Mts. Mongolia **46 B8** 46.30N 93.30E
Altiplano f. Bolivia **70 C4** 18.00S 67.30W
Amazon r. Brazil **70 F7** 2.00S 50.00W
Amazon, Mouths of the f. Brazil **70 G8** 0.00 50.00W
'Ammãn Jordan **42 C4** 31.57N 35.56E
Amsterdam Neth. **30 D4** 52.22N 4.54E
Amur r. Russia **37 P3** 53.17N 140.00E
Anápolis Brazil **70 G4** 16.19S 48.58W
Anchorage U.S.A. **64 E9** 61.10N 150.00W
Andaman Is. India **43 I2** 12.00N 93.00E
Andaman Sea Indian Oc. **43 I2** 11.00N 96.00E
Andes mts. S. America **68 D5** 15.00S 74.00W
Andorra Europe **30 D3** 42.30N 1.32E
Angola Africa **57 E2** 12.00S 18.00E
Ankara Turkey **31 G2** 39.55N 32.50E
Anshan China **46 E8** 41.05N 122.58E
Antananarivo Madagascar **57 H3** 18.52S 47.30E

Antarctica 80
Antigua and Barbuda Lesser Antilles **68 E8**
  17.30N 61.49W
Antofagasta Chile **69 D4** 23.40S 70.23W
Aoraki / Mount Cook mtn. New Zealand **77 H1**
  43.36S 170.09E
Apennines mts. Italy **32 D6** 44.00N 11.00E
Appalachian Mts. U.S.A. **65 K6** 39.30N 78.00W
Arabian Sea Asia **42 F2** 19.00N 65.00E
Arafura Sea Austa. **76 D5** 9.00S 135.00E
Araguaína Brazil **70 G6** 7.16S 48.18W
Araguari Brazil **70 G4** 18.38S 48.13W
Aral Sea Asia **42 E5** 45.00N 60.00E
Arctic Ocean 81
Arequipa Peru **70 B4** 16.25S 71.32W
Argentina S. America **69 E3** 35.00S 65.00W
Arica Chile **68 D5** 18.30S 70.20W
Arkansas r. U.S.A. **65 J6** 33.50N 91.00W
Arkhangel'sk Russia **36 F4** 64.32N 41.10E
Armenia Asia **42 D5** 40.00N 45.00E
Arnhem Land f. Australia **76 D4** 13.00S 132.30E
Aruba i. Lesser Antilles **68 D8** 12.30N 70.00W
Arusha Tanzania **58 C4** 3.21S 36.40E
Ashford England **23 H3** 51.08N 0.53E
Ashgabat Turkmenistan **42 E4** 37.53N 58.21E
Asia 40–41
Asmara Eritrea **56 G6** 15.20N 38.58E
Astana Kazakhstan **36 I3** 51.09N 71.27E
Asunción Paraguay **69 F4** 25.15S 57.40W
Atacama Desert S. America **69 E3** 20.00S 69.00W
Athens Greece **30 F2** 37.59N 23.42E
Atlanta U.S.A. **65 K6** 33.45N 84.23W
Atlantic Ocean 82 G7
Atlas Mts. Africa **56 C8** 33.00N 4.00W
Auckland New Zealand **77 H2** 36.52S 174.45E
Australia Austa. **76** 25.00S 135.00E
Austria Europe **30 E3** 47.30N 14.00E
Ayers Rock see Uluru Australia **76**
Ayr Scotland **24 D2** 55.28N 4.37W
Azerbaijan Asia **42 D5** 40.10N 47.50E
Azov, Sea of Ukraine **31 G3** 46.00N 36.30E

B

Baffin B. Canada **64 M10** 74.00N 70.00W
Baffin I. Canada **64 L9** 68.50N 70.00W
Baghdãd Iraq **42 D4** 33.20N 44.26E
Bahrain Asia **42 E3** 26.00N 50.35E

Baikal, L. Russia **37 L3** 53.30N 108.00E
Baja California pen. Mexico **65 H5** 27.00N 113.00W
Baku Azerbaijan **42 D5** 40.22N 49.53E
Balbina, Represa de resr. Brazil **70 E7** 1.30S 60.00W
Balearic Is. Spain **30 D2** 39.30N 2.30E
Balkan Mts. Bulgaria **30 F3** 42.50N 24.30E
Balkhash, L. Kazakhstan **36 I2** 46.51N 75.00E
Baltic Sea Europe **30 E4** 56.30N 19.00E
Baltimore U.S.A. **64 L6** 39.18N 76.38W
Bamako Mali **56 C6** 12.40N 7.59W
Bandar Seri Begawan Brunei **47 D4** 4.56N 114.58E
Bangkok Thailand **47 C5** 13.45N 100.35E
Bangladesh Asia **43 H3** 24.00N 90.00E
Bangui C.A.R. **56 E5** 4.23N 18.37E
Baotou China **46 D8** 40.38N 109.59E
Barbados Lesser Antilles **68 F8** 13.20N 59.40W
Barcelona Spain **30 D3** 41.25N 2.10E
Barents Sea Arctic Oc. **36 F5** 73.00N 40.00E
Barquisimeto Venezuela **68 E8** 10.03N 69.18W
Barranquilla Colombia **68 D8** 11.00N 74.50W
Basel Switz. **30 D3** 47.33N 7.36E
Bass Str. Australia **76 E2** 39.45S 146.00E
Bath England **23 E3** 51.22N 2.22W
Beijing China **46 D7** 39.55N 116.25E
Beirut Lebanon **42 C4** 33.52N 35.30E
Belarus Europe **30 E4** 52.32N 28.00E
Belém Brazil **70 G7** 1.27S 48.29W
Belfast N. Ireland **25 F4** 54.36N 5.57W
Belgium Europe **30 D4** 51.00N 4.30E
Belgrade Serb. **30 F3** 44.49N 20.28E
Belize C. America **65 K4** 17.00N 88.30W
Belmopan Belize **65 K4** 17.25N 88.46W
Belo Horizonte Brazil **71 H4** 19.45S 43.53W
Ben Nevis mtn. Scotland **24 D3** 56.48N 5.00W
Bengal, B. of Indian Oc. **43 H2** 17.00N 89.00E
Bengaluru India **43 G2** 12.58N 77.35E
Benin Africa **56 D5** 9.00N 2.30E
Benin, Bight of b. Africa **56 D5** 5.30N 3.00E
Bergen Norway **30 D5** 60.23N 5.20E
Bering Sea N. America/Asia **41 N6** 60.00N 170.00W
Berlin Germany **30 E4** 52.32N 13.25E
Bermuda i. Atlantic Oc. **65 M6** 32.18N 65.00W
Bern Switz. **30 D3** 46.57N 7.26E
Berwick-upon-Tweed England **22 E7**
  55.46N 2.00W
Bhutan Asia **43 I3** 27.25N 90.00E
Bié Plateau f. Angola **57 E3** 13.00S 16.00E

Birmingham England **23 F4** 52.30N 1.55W
Biscay, B. of France **30 C3** 45.30N 3.00W
Bishkek Kyrgyzstan **43 G5** 42.54N 74.32E
Bissau Guinea-Bissau **56 B6** 11.52N 15.39W
Black Sea Europe **31 G3** 43.00N 35.00E
Blackburn England **22 E5** 53.44N 2.30W
Blackpool England **22 D5** 53.48N 3.03W
Blanc, Mont mtn. Europe **30 D3** 45.50N 6.52E
Bloemfontein S. Africa **57 F2** 29.07S 26.13E
Bogotá Colombia **68 D7** 4.38N 74.05W
Bolivia S. America **68 E5** 17.00S 65.00W
Bologna Italy **32 D6** 44.30N 11.20E
Bolton England **22 E5** 53.35N 2.26W
Bombay see Mumbai India **43**
Bonn Germany **30 D4** 50.44N 7.06E
Bordeaux France **30 C3** 44.50N 0.34W
Borneo i. Asia **47 D4** 1.00N 114.00E
Bosnia and Herzegovina Europe **30 E3**
  44.00N 18.00E
Boston U.S.A. **64 L7** 42.15N 71.05W
Bothnia, G. of Europe **30 E5** 63.30N 20.30E
Botswana Africa **57 F2** 22.00S 24.00E
Bournemouth England **23 F2** 50.43N 1.53W
Bradford England **22 F5** 53.47N 1.45W
Brasília Brazil **70 G4** 15.54S 47.50W
Bratislava Slovakia **30 E3** 48.10N 17.10E
Brazil S. America **70–71** 10.00S 52.00W
Brazilian Highlands Brazil **70 G5** 17.00S 48.00W
Brazzaville Congo **56 E4** 4.14S 15.14E
Brighton England **23 G2** 50.50N 0.09W
Brisbane Australia **76 F3** 27.30S 153.00E
Bristol England **23 E3** 51.26N 2.35W
Bristol Channel England/Wales **23 C3**
  51.17N 3.20W
British Isles Europe **26 D5** 54.00N 5.00W
Brunei Asia **47 D4** 4.56N 114.58E
Brussels Belgium **30 D4** 50.50N 4.23E
Bucharest Romania **30 F3** 44.25N 26.06E
Budapest Hungary **30 E3** 47.30N 19.03E
Buenos Aires Argentina **69 F3** 34.40S 58.30W
Bujumbura Burundi **58 A4** 3.22S 29.21E
Bulgaria Europe **30 F3** 42.30N 25.00E
Burkina Faso Africa **56 C6** 12.15N 1.30W
Burma see Myanmar Asia **43**
Bursa Turkey **30 F3** 40.11N 29.04E
Burundi Africa **58 A4** 3.30S 30.00E
Busan S. Korea **46 E7** 35.05N 129.02E